B680 Certificate in Accounting

The O

- 2 OCT 2007

North Region

Supplementary Readings

OU Business School

Certificate in Accounting

Course Team
Judy Day, *Course Team and Block 1 Chair*
Sally Aisbitt, *Course Team Member*
Sam Cooper, *Regional Co-ordinator*
Devendra Kodwani, *Block 3 Chair*
Angelika Luetzow, *Course Manager*
Jean Rowe, *Course Team Assistant*
Sharon Slade, *Regional Manager*
Jonathan Winship, *Block 2 Chair*

Authors
Sally Aisbitt
Haider Ali
David Barnes
Bernardo Bátiz-Lazo
Mary Bowerman
Philip Cahill
Judy Day
Michael Dempsey
Nancy Finlay
Graham Francis
Stephen Little
Andrew Lymer
Clare Minchington
Sue Pearce
Alan Sangster
Philip Talbot
David Tyrrall

External Assessor
Professor Richard M.S.Wilson,
Loughborough University Business School

Subject Specific Assessors
Stephen Barr
David Crowther
Neil Marriott
Jayne Smith
Greg Stoner

Production
Paul Beeby, *Project Manager*
Holly Clements, *Media Assistant*
Lene Connolly, *Print Buyer*
Jonathan Davies, *Graphic Designer*
Diane Hopwood, *Compositor*
Jonathan Owen, *Graphic Artist*
Dave Pilgrim, *Web Developer*
Nikki Smith, *Assistant Print Buyer*
Jill Somerscales, *Editor*

Critical Readers
Vicki Amos, Ian Apps, Adrian Bolton, Don Cooper, Michael Dempsey, Charles Edwards, Mark Fenton-O'Creevy, Jayne Hughes, Alva James, Archie McArthur, Kieran McKenna, Elizabeth Porter, Charles Rush, Steve Tossell, Peter Trowell and Christopher Worthington.

Developmental Testers
David Attenborough, Mary Caffrey, John Copas, Moira Deakins, Linda Hadfield, Lesley Messer, Rawdon O'Connor and Brenda Peers-Ross.

Software
Software for the Course was designed, adapted and remains the property of EQL Ltd.
Accounting package software was designed, adapted and remains the property of Sage plc.
Assessment software from Question*mark* Computing Ltd.

Other Course Material
The Course Team wishes to acknowledge use of existing course material from a number of OUBS courses.

Contents

1.1 Accounting for growth I

Terry Smith

Introduction

> *Definition of a recession: A time when money is returned to its rightful owners*
> Anon

Why write another book on accounting? A visit to the Business section of any bookshop reveals a wealth of textbooks on the subject. There are several reasons for writing this particular book:

Since I began working in finance during the Secondary Banking Crisis and recession of 1973–75 I have continually been challenged by friends outside the City with a question which goes something like 'XYZ company went bust last week, but it was making profits. How can that happen?' The first example of such questions I can recall was the collapse of a retailer called Brentford Nylons in February 1976. The company had a high profile as a cut-price high street retailer whose TV advertising featured a well-known disc jockey, Alan Freeman, so its collapse attracted attention from many people outside the financial services industry. It is to those people in part that this book is directed – to help answer the questions so often posed of how a company reporting profits can still go bust. Brentford Nylons was a private company. Its last accounts prior to going into receivership were for 1974, when profits of £130,000 were recorded, but only after a special credit of £550,000 in respect of a claim against a supplier, and receipt of a regional development grant of £180,000. There is nothing new about creative accounting. Incidentally, for antiquarians amongst you, Brentford Nylons was ultimately taken over by Lonrho.

Secondly, it became apparent that the recession of 1990–91 was producing a similar effect in that some companies reporting record profits were almost simultaneously going into administration. Probably the most dramatic example from the point of view of the speed of the collapse is Polly Peck, which is dealt with in the following section, 'How could it happen?' and in more detail in Appendix III. And there are plenty of other examples of companies going bust in this recession which reported 'profits' in their last results announcements and accounts – British & Commonwealth, BCCI, Maxwell Communications. To deal with some of the issues of accounting which were being raised by the events of the 1990/92 recession Richard Hannah, the Transport analyst at UBS Phillips & Drew, and I co-authored a report entitled *Accounting for Growth* at the beginning of 1991.

The title *Accounting for Growth* was a deliberate pun. We felt that much of the apparent growth in profits which has occurred in the 1980s was the result of accounting sleight of hand rather than genuine economic growth, and we set out to expose the main techniques involved, and to give live examples of companies using those techniques.

Accounting for Growth was sent to UBS Phillips & Drew's institutional clients and we presented the report to more than 60 of them. We found a surprising thirst for information in this area, particularly when it is allied to live examples. So much so that the original report was voted the best piece of research published during 1991 in the Extel survey of institutional investors. What this volume attempts to do is expand on the original work and in particular to go further into each company example, where possible reproducing the relevant section from Annual Report and Accounts so that readers can see where to find the information and how to perform the calculations needed to spot creative accounting techniques.

Is *Accounting for Growth* intended to help you make money? I start from the standpoint that few, if any, of us would read books on finance without this aim in mind, although it is probably fairer to say that this book is intended to prevent you from losing money in investment. The original research publication had a chapter entitled Major Companies Accounting Health Check, which is reproduced and updated in Chapter 16. This looked at over 200 UK companies listed on the International Stock Exchange and indicated where they were using one of the accounting/financial engineering techniques identified in the report. This checklist became affectionately know as the 'blob guide' because a blob or mark was placed in the appropriate column for each technique used by a company. Unfortunately no method of ranking the degree of a company's use of a particular technique could be found despite some heroic failures in the attempt to compute a scoring system. It always came down to a matter of judgement whether one company's change in depreciation policy was more or less serious than another's currency mismatching. We were therefore left with the simplest guide of all: the number of techniques (or number of blobs) used by each company. Since the publication of the original report this remarkably simple technique has proved to be an amazingly accurate guide to the companies to avoid as Table 1.1 shows.

The table shows all the companies with five or more blobs i.e. using five or more of the 11 accounting and financing techniques surveyed in *Accounting for Growth*. With the notable exceptions of Dixons and Next, which performed well in 1991, the share price performance of the other companies has ranged from indifferent to disastrous, with Maxwell Communications Corporation representing a near certain total loss to shareholders.

So if in doubt about the accounting don't hold the shares

Which brings us to practical advice on the layout of this book and how to read it. Parts II and III detail the techniques of accounting and financial engineering which have proved most frequent and pernicious. Part IV is the Major Companies Accounting Health Check (or 'blob guide') updated for current events and also has a

Table 1.1 Share price performance of the high scorers in Accounting for Growth Mk. I		
	Number of 'Blobs'	**Relative share price performance in 1991%**
LEP	5	−90
Maxwell	7	−100 (suspended)
ASDA	5	−66
British Aerospace	7	−44
Burton	7	−43
Ultramar*	5	−16
Blue Circle	5	−10
Cable & Wireless	6	−5
Granada	5	−4
Sears	5	−4
Laporte	5	+6
Dixons	6	+40
Next	5	+234
* *After* bid from Lasmo		

chapter entitled Survival Techniques in the Accounting Jungle. For company accounting, like the investment industry or the dealing room of a major securities firm, is a jungle with many species of animal – some benign, some carnivorous – and its own rules. Anyone who believes this is an exaggeration should read one of the entertaining studies of the securities industry, perhaps most notably Michael Lewis's *Liar's Poker* (Hodder & Stoughton, 1989) about events and personalities at Salomon Brothers, including John Gutfreund and John Meriwether, the Chairman and head of bond trading who both left Salomons after the revelations about bids at US Government bond auctions.

The Survival Techniques chapter is intended to give some simple and some unorthodox rules about reading a set of company annual accounts which might ensure that the reader is not caught up in the gloss of the annual accounts and can separate 'profit' from cash. Reverting to the Brentford Nylons example with which this Introduction began, this is the key distinction. The word 'profit' has been placed in inverted commas for good reasons – it's the result of the accountants' 'true and fair view' or, to give it its less polite name, a guess. What we would call 'an opinion' in plain English. Whereas cash is a fact. And cash is ultimately what makes or breaks a business, and this distinction is the one that my questioners could not grasp back in the recession of 1973, but which you must now learn if you are to survive in the Accounting Jungle. Good luck and good hunting.

How could it happen?

Polly Peck

On Monday 3 September 1990, Polly Peck International, the food and consumer electronics group, reported its Interim profit figures for the half year to 30 June 1990. Pre-tax profits were £110.5m, well up from £64.4m in the first half of 1989, as were Earnings Per Share of 22.4p (17.8p) and the Interim dividend of 5.5p net (4.5p). At this point Polly Peck was capitalized by the London stock market at £1.05bn. It had interests in quoted subsidiaries, Sansui and Vestel, electronics companies listed in Tokyo and Istanbul, valued at £660m, and had recently acquired the fresh food interests of Del Monte. The Interim Balance Sheet showed shareholders' funds of £932.7m – nearly one billion pounds.

The only cloud on the horizon was a strange episode in which Asil Nadir, Polly Peck's high profile Chairman, had recently made an approach aimed at acquiring the company's shares from other shareholders in a bid to 'take it private'. This was just the sort of move which had been seen across the Atlantic in the Management Buy-Out (MBO)/Leveraged Buy-Out (LBO) boom of recent years. But Nadir had decided not to proceed with his bid approach and had attracted some speculation on the reasons why, and why he had launched it, not to mention criticism from the Quotations Panel of the International Stock Exchange about the manner of his approach and its announcement.

How could it be that just over two weeks later at 2.21pm on Thursday 20 September, trading in Polly Peck's shares was suspended after the share price plunged by 135p to 108p? The immediate cause was a search hours earlier of the offices of South Audley Management, a company connected with Asil Nadir, by members of the Serious Fraud Office (SFO). In August 1990, Polly Peck's shares had peaked at 457p, valuing the company at £1784m. They were now on their way to becoming worthless.

On Thursday 25 October, one month later, partners of Cork Gully and Cooper & Lybrand were appointed as administrators for Polly Peck. During a High Court hearing, the results of an insolvency study by Coopers & Lybrand were revealed allegedly showing that an immediate liquidation of Polly Peck would produce a deficit for shareholders of £384m.

How could it happen? There are many explanations which can be proffered: obviously liquidation values are not the same as going concern values in a Balance Sheet and so on. But the fact is that in a period of about six months Polly Peck had changed from a darling of the stock market, reporting record profits, with Shareholders' funds of nearly £1bn and a market value which peaked a month earlier at £1.75 billion, into an insolvent company whose shareholders' investment has probably been wiped out. It is this sort of contradiction, and the inability of investors to understand what happened, which brings accounting and stock markets into disrepute.

The UK entered into a recession in the third quarter of 1990, and many public companies have since gone bust, but Polly Peck's demise should not be lost in this welter of failures. Its interests were mostly outside the UK, so it was not caught in the dramatic slowdown induced in the UK economy as an antidote to the Lawson boom.

Polly Peck is probably the most dramatic example of the large company collapses of this period, partly because of the legal proceedings against Chairman Asil Nadir, but also because of the sheer speed of its demise. (A longer review of Polly Peck's rise and fall is given in Appendix III.) But it is not the only large company to suffer this apparently inexplicable fate at this time ...

British & Commonwealth

British & Commonwealth's (B&C's) demise was not as rapid or so apparently unexpected as that of Polly Peck, but if anything, it fell from a greater height. At the peak of its share price in July 1987, B&C was valued at £1853m, making it the 46th largest company in the UK by market value, and the second largest financial company after the venerable Prudential.

By the time B&C's last set of results were announced on 27 September 1989, problems were already apparent. Not only were profits (before goodwill amortisation) down from £82.9m to £60.3m, but B&C was also experiencing difficulty disposing of some of the superfluous businesses it had acquired with Mercantile House in 1987, such as MW Marshal & Co. the money brokers, and fatefully it had acquired Atlantic Computers a year earlier in September 1988.

On 17 April 1990, the first day back to work for the City after a Bank holiday, B&C's shares were suspended at 53p. At a hastily convened analysts' meeting at the Waldorf Hotel, new Chairman Sir Peter Thompson, who had been brought in from the highly successful NFC (the flotation of National Freight Consortium which had been an MBO from BR) attempted to explain what had gone wrong. At this point the main problem was idetified as the liabilities of B&C's computer leasing subsidiary Atlantic Computers, which was to be 'ring fenced' or, less politely, B&C was to rely upon the principle of limited liability by allowing its subsidiary to go into administration.

Unfortunately, or fortunately depending upon your point of view, this ploy did not work and B&C itself went into administration on 3 June 1990.

(A more detailed study of B&C's complex life and times is included in Appendix II.)

Coloroll

Coloroll was not as big as B&C, nor was its end as speedy and unexpected as Polly Peck's. But it is still worth studying as one of the major failures of this era of the late 1980s. At its peak in June 1988, Coloroll had been valued at £424m.

Coloroll's last profit announcement was on 16 November 1989 and, once again, it was already apparent that everything was not well. Pre-tax profits fell from £20.55m to £10.01m. Factory closures and redundancies characterised the results statement, and as *Marketing Magazine* put it, 'when Coloroll, the notoriously bullish home products group, starts talking about "organic consolidation" times are getting tough'. Gearing was stated at 75 per cent, although this was much less than the reality (see Appendix I).

The shares were suspended and administrative receivers were appointed on 7 June 1990.

How could it happen?

These three large corporate collapses all owe their occurrence in some respects to techniques of creative accounting or financial engineering. The relevant chapters for analysing the techniques they used in the section on Accounting Techniques which follows are:

Polly Peck – Currency Mismatching (Chapter 15)

British & Commonwealth – Acquisition and disposal techniques (Chapters 3–6)

Contingent liabilities (Chapter 9)

Coloroll – Acquisition and disposal techniques (Chapters 3–6)

Maxwell

But probably the greatest puzzle is how events at the late Robert Maxwell's empire were allowed to develop to the point where the two quoted companies in Maxwell's control were in the following (estimated) position after his demise:

Maxwell Communications Corporation (MCC)

MCC had net debts of around £1.5bn against net assets of under £1bn. It has already filed for Chapter 11 liquidationcy protection in the United States, and an administrator has been appointed in the UK. MCC's shares are almost certainly worthless, having fallen from a peak of 241p in 1991 to a price of $77\frac{1}{2}$p at which they were suspended.

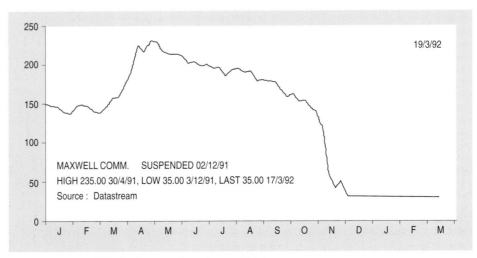

Figure 1.1   MCC share price chart 1991

Mirror Group Newspapers (MGN)

Some £97m has disappeared from MGN's bank account and was transferred to Maxwell's private companies, and £350m is missing from its pension fund, turning a £150m surplus into a £110m deficit.

But despite the enormity of the sums involved, and the complex daisy chain of 400 companies involved in the Maxwell group, Maxwell's action was 'not sophisticated fraud' (*Financial Times* 7.12.91). The methods by which Maxwell misappropriated hundreds of millions of pounds were:

1 Pledging assets and then selling them rather than delivering them to lender as security – this occurred more than once in Maxwell's empire: i) the 'sale' of the Berlitz language school to Fukutake, a Japanese publishing company, when the shares had already been pledged as security for loans by Swiss Volksbank and Lehman Brothers to Robert Maxwell Group, and ii) a £57.5m loan from Swiss Bank Corporation to a private Maxwell Company to finance a bid for First Tokyo Index Trust, which was to be secured by the Japanese shares held by the Trust. But the shares were sold, and the proceeds diverted elsewhere.

2 Plundering the pension funds – Maxwell diverted shares and cash held by Mirror Group Newspapers' £400m pension fund from outside advisers such as Lazards, Capel Cure Myers, and Lloyds Investment Managers to Bishopsgate Investment Management, a privately owned Maxwell company. The assets of the pension funds were then pledged as security for loans to other Maxwell companies.

3 Share support operations – part of the collateral for the lending to Maxwell's private interests was the security which he gave the bankers in the form of a mortgage over his shares in the quoted vehicles – MCC and MGN. But when his empire began to run into trouble the share prices came under pressure and he faced the possibility of margin calls from his bankers which he could not meet. Consequently, Maxwell used the cash raised by other methods to purchase more shares in MCC and MGN, so supporting the price. The problem here is twofold: i) he never disclosed the increase in his shareholding in accordance with Companies Act and Stock Exchange requirements, so misleading investors about the reasons for the rise in share price. Thus, Maxwell private companies had a disclosed interest of 67.7 per cent in MCC, but actually controlled more than 80 per cent and ii) the companies were effectively funding the purchase of their own shares – a practice forbidden by the Companies Acts, except in certain limited circumstances, and the offence which was at the centre of the Guinness trials.

Funds of £130m from Maxwell Group, Bishopsgate Investment Trust and London and Bishopsgate Group, private Maxwell companies, were used to buy MCC shares in April and July 1991.

Perhaps the most sophisticated element of the operation was that in which Maxwell sold put options in MCC shares to investment bankers Goldman Sachs in August 1990 and July 1991 at prices higher than those then ruling in the market. This meant that Goldman had the right to sell the shares to Maxwell under the put option and could then buy in the market at lower prices, thereby showing a profit. Maxwell thereby indirectly supported the price, and increased his stake in MCC.

4   Simply taking the cash – in the months after MGN's flotation, MGN 'lent' £43m to private Maxwell companies. This £45m was part of MGN's cash resources which MGN instructed the Maxwell companies to invest in gilt-edged stocks as an alternative to holding cash. But of course the gilts were never purchased.

And all of this happened to a company which was a member of the FTSE 100 Index of the largest quoted companies – which is often assumed by many, especially foreign investors, to represent 'blue chip' companies.

But is attention to accounting any safeguard to investors against becoming involved in a company which is subject to a scandal that is the 'daddy of them all' (Ivon Fallon, *Sunday Times*, 8 December 1991)? In the original *Accounting for Growth* publication, Maxwell Communications Corporation was one of the only three companies to receive seven 'blobs' for the use of creative accounting techniques in the Major Companies Accounting Health Check:

Perhaps it should have been called a Wealth Check!

Source: Smith, T. (1992) *Accounting for Growth: Stripping the Camouflage from Company Accounts*, London, Century Business, 1st Edn, Ch. 1–2, pp. 3–12

1.2 Accounting for growth II

Terry Smith

A funny thing happened on the way to the publishers

Hollow vessels make the greatest sound
Anon

That plus 10 cents and you get a ride on the subway
New Yorkers' saying

It may help to bring readers up to date about this book if I begin with some of the extraordinary events in the summer of 1992. After the original research report in early 1991, preparation of the book and publication went ahead uneventfully and do not deserve comment. It was not publication that caused the excitement in 1992, but the attempts to suppress the book completely.

I have already explained in the first edition how I was prompted to write the book by the even more extraordinary events in the UK economy and stock market in 1990–92. In my opinion, these events were due to more than just the impact of a ferocious recession given additional impetus by the reaction to events in Kuwait in the summer of 1990. UK quoted companies had begun to drop like ninepins, and I was struck by the extent to which investors, even professional fund managers and analysts, were quite naïve in thinking that published company accounts were in some way a protection against losing money in this maelstrom. I am producing a second and updated edition because I am not much less impressed by their naïveté today, as you will see from the BTR example which I quote in Chapter 4 and on page 189.

I wrote the book in a particular format: with lots of examples taken from company accounts. There had been works on creative accounting before, such as Ian Griffiths' *Creative Accounting* but they had generally failed to name names, relying instead upon using examples of 'Company A' and 'Company B'. I felt that readers should be able to use the book to look at live (and dead) company examples in order to give them a realistic guide as to what to look for. This presented an obvious problem. The original report had caused some stirrings in the undergrowth from companies which were unhappy about being included. Now some were alerted to the fact that there was a book on the way.

After the manuscript has been completed, submitted to the publishers and proof-read, the attempt to suppress the book took off. The first contact was from Tiphook, the container leasing company which had featured in the original research report and was now in the book. Representations were made by Tiphook's Chairman, Robert Montagu ([Tiphook] subsequently declared in liquidation) to suggest that Tiphook should be dropped as an example. [Please note that, in the UK, the terminology is that a firm or company goes into liquidation whereas, in the US, a firm is said to go bankrupt.]

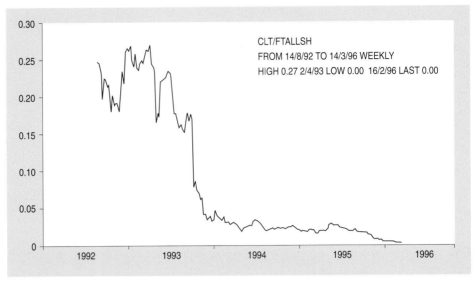

CLT/FTALLSH
FROM 14/8/92 TO 14/3/96 WEEKLY
HIGH 0.27 2/4/93 LOW 0.00 16/2/96 LAST 0.00

Figure 1.1 *Tiphook (Central Transport Rental) share price relative to the All Share Index 1992–96*

But Montagu did not have enough clout to cause a real problem. That came when Grand Met discovered from preliminary press reviews that it was the company with the most 'blobs' in the notorious 'Major Companies Accounting Health Check' table, or as it became known, the Blob Guide. Out of twelve techniques examined in the first edition, Grand Met was listed as using nine, the largest number for any company in the Top 200. It is a supreme irony that after the first edition was published and I was fired and sued I had to check the accuracy of a number of entries including Grand Met's and found that I had missed one: Grand Met was using ten techniques!

Grand Met took a dim view of this and pressure was bought to bear by Allen Shepherd and, when this did not succeed, by Colin Marshall, a non-executive director of Grand Met, but more crucially, then Chief Executive of British Airways. I was then told to stop publication of the book completely. Apart from my wishes in the matter, everyone seemed to have overlooked a small difficulty in achieving this: it was no longer my book and I had no control over it. I had already sold the book to my publisher. He now both possessed and owned the book, and owed me royalties. Contacting a publisher and asking him to stop publication was not only a highly unusual step for an author to take, it was also likely to make him (or her) have the commercial equivalent of an orgasm. Publicity sells books (some people seemed to have overlooked the common roots between the words 'publisher' and 'publicity') as anyone who had followed the case of the British Government's attempts to block the publication of *Spycatcher* would have known. Telling a publisher not to publish because there was a row brewing was a bit like giving someone a tanker full of petrol with which to extinguish a fire. Whoosh!

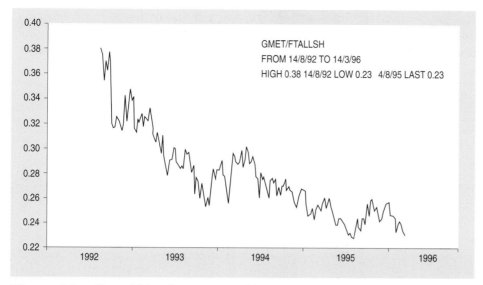

Figure 1.2   *Grand Met share price relative to the All Share Index 1992–96*

The rest, as they say, is history. The book was published. I was fired and sued. The book received more publicity than Random House could probably have purchased with its entire advertising budget. Analysts woke up to the issue of creative accounting in general, and in companies such as Grand Met and Tiphook in particular:

A very curious episode in my life then unfolded. Apart from deciding what to do for the rest of my working life, and fighting a substantial lawsuit, I was also engaged on a speaking tour which took me around the UK and to Ireland and France, speaking about creative accounting. This was enjoyable, but some curious episodes occurred. I refer in particular to one conference at which I was confronted by a speaker from accountants Ernst & Young. Ernst & Young were the only firm which had gone on record at the time of publication to condemn the book as 'dangerous and irresponsible'. The press seemed to have overlooked the coincidence that Ernst & Young were a) UBS's auditors; and b) the only firm of accountants named in the book. It is amazing how these coincidences go unremarked: UBS became brokers to Tiphook after I was fired, despite the fact that their Transport analyst (one Richard Hannah would you believe, the co-author of the original 'Accounting for Growth' research report) had been a constant critic of the company. Anyway, the Ernst & Young speaker proceeded to berate me for producing a book that was inaccurate and too simplistic. In its place he recommended Ernst & Young's publication *UK GAAP* ('Generally Accepted Accounting Practice') the current edition of which ran to some 1,226 pages of technical analysis.

When I was able to set aside my feeling of surprise that any UK accountant should have the gall to criticise someone else's work as misleading in the light of various episodes concerning the accountancy profession in recent years which are almost too numerous to mention, I was able to agree that *UK GAAP* and a host of other books are much better technical guides to UK accounting than *Accounting for Growth*. My reason for labouring this incident is that I want the opportunity to reiterate the reasons behind the publication of this book and its target audience in this second edition. At its simplest, if I wanted to write a book on accounting which was useful to senior technical partners of Ernst & Young, my royalty account would be a lot smaller. Moreover, I wanted to write a book that would help laymen to understand what was going on. The average person who is sufficiently interested in investment to read a book on accounting is not likely to select a 1,226-page manual.

But there was an even more important difference from *UK GAAP* and *Accounting for Growth* which the man from Ernst & Young seemed to miss, in common with a lot of professionals. A frequent defence which is heard when any company's accounting is criticised is "but it [the treatment being adopted] is allowed within UK GAAP."

To my knowledge none of the companies named in the first edition nor any of the companies in this second edition are in breach of UK GAAP in the treatments they are using and which I highlight. But as they say in New York "that plus 10 cents and you get a ride on the subway". Or to put in English; so what? It is quite possible to lose money if a company's accounts follow UK GAAP to the letter, but the picture presented is so misleading that you are unable to interpret them correctly and as a result fail to see that it is financially vulnerable or its earnings are unsustainable.

As anyone who has read the first edition will know, in this book I try to give a quote at the beginning of each chapter which gives some clue to is contents. Well at least now you know the context to the second quote for this chapter, but what about empty vessels making the greatest sound? The share price charts for Tiphook and Grand Met obviously give me some pride, and not just because their executives caused me some needless problems. I also got some clients to sell shares and so avoid losses. A book is not a finely timed instrument like a piece of broker's research which can be produced literally overnight, and may have a very short shelf life. The predictions and rules in a book may take longer to work, but they should also pass the test of time.

I must leave you, the reader, to decide whether this is true of *Accounting for Growth*, but with all due respect to the gentlemen (and ladies) from Ernst & Young I reproduce below an article from *The Sunday Times* in November 1993, which looks at the fate of some of the high scorers in the blob guide as a contribution to the debate. The 'blob guide' was never intended to be a precise instrument of analysis, since for example it makes no attempt to weight the size or impact of the accounting techniques utilised, and if anything I am surprised at how successful it has been given these obvious limitations. It was only ever intended as a warning to the reader to examine the accounts of any company listed.

So how does this explain empty vessels? If I were running a public company, and some analyst decided to criticise my company's accounts, I like to believe that if I knew he was wrong I would not rail against him in public or call his boss and demand a retraction or his dismissal. Rather I would smile knowingly and hope the poor, misguided fellow drove the company's share price down so that I could buy a few more. In my experience, when companies start issuing threats, and bringing back door pressure to bear to stop criticism, this is a better indicator that something is wrong than all of the blob guides, UK GAAP books, analysts' circulars and charts put together.

Pleasant reading.

The maverick analyst who went to war with the City and won

Terry Smith was vilified for his book on company accounts. But the downfall of Queens Moat, Trafalgar and Tiphook has proved him right.

Fifteen months after Terry Smith's controversial book, Accounting for Growth, climbed into the bestseller lists, event after event is proving the maverick analyst right.

Three of the most notable corporate disasters of the year – Queens Moat Houses, the hotels group; Tiphook, the container and trailer rental company; and Trafalgar House, the contracting and construction firm now controlled by Hongkong Land – were highlighted in the book for their dubious accounting practices. Smith, now working at Collins Stewart, the boutique broker, can barely suppress a smile.

"Tiphook, if you look back on it, was frighteningly obvious," he says. "The amazing thing is that UBS then took the company on as a client."

UBS, the Swiss bank where Smith was the head of research until he was removed from the premises after refusing to scrap his book, is pressing ahead with its case for alleged breach of copyright. Smith has responded with a claim for unfair dismissal. The bank denies it objected to the book because of pressure from clients, and claims Smith broke house rules by failing to check the facts with the companies concerned before publishing.

A trial is due to begin next October, and "discovery" of documents continued in the High Court last week.

Smith has spent an estimated £170,000 on legal bills and, with Singer & Friedlander, the merchant bank, offering financial backing, is ready and willing to press on. His financial resources are meagre against those of UBS, one of the world's banking giants, but UBS has discovered its opponent is nothing if not determined. Sources say attempts by the Swiss bank to settle out of court have been turned down.

Smith is keeping a close eye on the companies that he says tried to intervene to have the book abandoned or their names deleted from it.

"It is fascinating to watch the performance of those companies that tried to get the book stopped," he says. Sir Allen Sheppard's Grand Metropolitan, which topped Smith's list for the highest number of dubious accounting methods, was among those to complain to UBS. "Since then Grand Met shares have significantly underperformed the rest of the market," he points out.

Inntrepreneur, GrandMet's pub joint venture with Courage, now finds its loans listed by at least one merchant back as "distressed debt", selling for only a portion of their full face value, a status usually reserved for companies acknowledged to be facing financial difficulties. Debt in the loss-making Inntrepreneur does not sell at the heavy discounts to book value reached by Gerald Ronson's Heron Group, for example, but Smith believes Inntrepreneur's debt is uncomfortably high.

Robert Montagu, chairman of Tiphook, was another to express his unhappiness. Tiphook is now holding talks with its bankers after gearing soared to more than 500%.

How Smith's culprits came unstuck

Companies using the most dubious accounting practices

Tiphook (4)	In talks with banks, debts soar
Queens Moat (6)	Financial reconstruction under way
Trafalgar House (8)	Auditors, chairman and chief executive depart; huge losses, two rights issues
Albert Fisher (7)	Losses, chairman departs
British Aerospace (7)	Record losses, rights issue
Ratners (7)	Founder departs, huge losses
Lonrho (6)	Huge changes in way groups is run
GrandMet (9)	Shares underperform
Bass (6)	Shares underperform
Ladbroke (8)	Chairman steps down

Trafalgar House became one of the highest-profile cases of dubious accounting when it was forced to re-issue accounts after a protracted inquiry by the Financial Review Panel.

When first published, Smith's book was criticised as superficial and an unreliable guide to company accounts. Ernst & Young, an accountant with several clients among Smith's list of worst offenders, dismissed the book as "dangerous and irresponsible". Others (including The Sunday Times, which published extracts), welcomed Smith's method of bringing the usually dry issue of accountancy methods into the open.

"Terry identified exactly the same problems as we did with the accountancy world," says Professor David Tweedie, head of the Accounting Standards Board. "I think of the 12 issues highlighted we have now dealt with nine of them." Certainly investors who avoided companies covered in the book would be much better off today.

In his new job, Smith now specialises in targeting and analysing companies that may be facing financial difficulties.

Just over a year ago, Smith questioned the apparent infallibility of Spring Ram, then a highly successfully kitchens and bathrooms group. This year, the edifice began to crumble and the company is now facing severe financial difficulties. "There were some very obvious superficial signals that the company had lost touch with its business," he says. "The annual report was full of sportsmen wearing Spring Ram shirts, but there were no pictures of bathrooms."

A trigger for further investigations is high profit margins. "If they are achieving improbable margins they are probably doing something wrong. There has to be a logical explanation." Polly Peck was an obvious example.

A company to watch, he suggests, is BTR, because it is muddying its accounting methods rather than cleaning them up. "We all understood where BTR used to get its 15% margins from because they were outstanding industrial managers," he says. "But the acquisition accounting on their purchase of Hawker Siddeley was as bad as I have ever seen. It is now like trying to view something through a smokescreen."

Article by Kirstie Hamilton, *The Sunday Times*, 14 November 1993

What has happened since 1992?

A girl writes home from her boarding school to her parents. Her letter tells them that there has been a fire in her dormitory. Her parents are obviously worried by this news. But the letter goes on to say that she was rescued by the school handyman. She has forged a strong friendship with the handyman as a result. So strong in fact that she is pregnant by him and they have eloped. Her parents are aghast until they read the postscript which says "None of the foregoing actually happened. I just failed my History GCSE and wanted you to get it into perspective."

Joke told by Sir David Tweedie, Chairman of the ASB. The punchline is always 'Look at the bottom line' including in letters.

It brings home the need for this second edition for me to realise that the Accounting Standards Board (ASB) had only just issued its first Financial Reporting Standards (FRS) – FRS 1 when the first edition was published. In fact a question which I have often been asked at seminars and conferences is something along the lines of: is there really any need for your book now that we have the ASB? To some extent, this new edition attempts to answer that question by looking at the state of company accounting after all the ASB achieved.

The foundation of the ASB under Sir David Tweedie was a recognition that there was a great deal wrong with UK accounting. Tweedie has set about correcting this with an almost evangelical zeal. And he tells good jokes. It does not do full justice to his achievements at the ASB simply to list its published standards. But nonetheless here goes:

Financial Reporting Standards (FRS)	
FRS 1	Cash Flow Statements
FRS 2	Accounting for Subsidiary Undertakings
FRS 3	Reporting Financial Performance
FRS 4	Capital Instruments
FRS 5	Reporting the Substance of Transactions
FRS 6	Acquisitions and Mergers
FRS 7	Fair Values in Acquisition Accountancy
FRS 8	Related party disclosures

For the non-technical reader, the contents of some of these Standards is almost impossible to predict from the title. Take FRS 3. 'Reporting Financial Performance' could cover almost anything.

Many of this series of new FRS relate precisely to areas mentioned in the first edition, and will be covered in some detail in the following chapters. There are also a number of discussion papers and exposure drafts which will become new Standards, such as those dealing with pension funds, goodwill and deferred taxation; these are covered in the later chapters in which we look forward to new developments in accounting and the effects which they may have on companies.

In addition the Urgent Issues Task Force (UITF) has also issued Abstracts ostensibly clarifying existing standards, but in reality often changing the way companies are able to draw up their accounts in response to some of the grosser abuses which have been perpetrated. Two that we shall look at which have had a profound effect are UITF Abstract 3: Treatment of goodwill on disposal of a business, and Abstract 5: Transfers from current assets to fixed assets.

It is not, however, the aim of this second edition to stand in judgement on the ASB's work, but rather just to update readers on some loopholes which have been closed since 1992, and some new ones which have opened. There is little doubt that the ASB has achieved a great deal in making UK accounting more rigorous, but there is equally little doubt that their task will never be finished in any normal sense. David Tweedie himself in his more candid moments confesses that his job is a bit like painting the Forth Bridge. Once it is finished you start all over again. He realised that whatever rules you put in place, smart people will find a way to express a distorted or flattering picture of their performance. He recognises that the ASB will in that sense always be one step behind. The Forth Bridge aspect of his work is brought home by the fact that as I prepare this second edition, the ASB has just issued FRED ('Financial Reporting Exposure Draft') 10 with it revisions to FRS 1. This is designed to solve some of the problems which quickly became apparent in the implementation of this first Standard. That if you like is the bottom line to what the ASB has achieved to date: better accounting standards, but they cannot remain ossified for all time, and neither could *Accounting for Growth*.

Some of the chapters from the first edition have been unaffected by the ASB's reforms, and so have survived almost in their entirety. These are: Deferred Consideration (Chapter 6); Contingent Liabilities (Chapter 9); Capitalisation of Costs (Chapter 10); Brand Accounting (Chapter 11); Changes in Depreciation Policy (Chapter 12); Currency Mismatching (Chapter 14) and Pension Fund Accounting (Chapter 15).

However, in some cases they have been modified to take account of developments since 1992. Examples are the chapter on Depreciation, which now includes some material on the debate about the depreciation of properties, and on Pension Fund Accounting which includes the proposals in the ASB's Discussion Paper. In other cases new examples have been introduced, such as the example of Quality Software Products in the chapter on Capitalisation of Costs and a review of information on Hanson's interest rate arbitrage activities in the chapter on Currency Mismatching.

Other chapters have ceased to have any significance as a result of the new Financial Reporting Standards. For example, FRS 3 basically outlawed extraordinary items and thereby rendered Chapter 7 in the first edition redundant. But it has been replaced by a new chapter on the operation of FRS 3. The reader will find that in common with other chapters, it does not give a detailed description of FRS 3. It is instead meant to serve as a short and hopefully readable guide to those aspects of the operation of FRS 3 which may affect the investor.

Similarly, all of the techniques described in the old chapters on Off Balance Sheet Finance and Convertibles With Put Options and AMPs have effectively been dealt with by FRS 2, FRS 4 and FRS 5. There are still companies with weird and wonderful capital instruments and assets and, more important, liabilities on off Balance Sheet structures. But reporting of these items has been tightened so that there is now less chance for companies to shift items off their reported group Balance Sheet, the main purpose of which is to understate the gearing. Beyond a certain point, the higher a company's gearing, the lower its equity should be rated because the existence of high gearing can be a threat to the equity holders' capital and income. For example, FRS 2 brought the definition of a subsidiary in accounting standards into line with the Companies Acts. It widened the definition of control to bring in the sort of 'non-subsidiary subsidiary' route used by the likes of LEP with St Pauls Vista (see chapter 8 in the first edition) with their property assets and borrowings back on to the group Balance Sheet, often with disastrous effects.

Some chapters have required heavy modification as a result of the ASB's reforms, such as the chapters on Acquisition Accounting and Disposals. The opportunity has also been taken to introduce new examples into these chapters from the period since 1992 in order to bring them up to date.

Chapters have also been introduced on entirely new areas of accounting which have become topical as a result of developments since 1992, such as Cash Flow Accounting, and Transfers from Current Assets to Fixed Assets.

In general, an effort has been made to shorten chapters since 1992. This is partly because accounting remains a subject which few people will read about for pleasure, so my view is that the less you have to read to get the essence of a subject, the better. But in contrast it is worth noting that there are chapters dealing with fifteen techniques of so-called creative accounting in this edition versus a dozen in 1992. Perhaps this is a reflection of the remaining opportunities to 'cook the books' even after all the ASB's reforms? It certainly emphasises the need for constant vigilance if you are not to be parted from your money.

After the chapters on creative techniques, the Major Companies Accounting Health Check has been dropped. Although it was a popular item in the 1992 edition and caused great controversy, it always suffered from the shortcomings of an admittedly simplistic approach. Instead, the chapter on Survival Techniques has been heavily modified with some of the previous hints, such as watching for transfers between the Balance Sheet and Profit and Loss Account and cash flow, given chapters of their own in order to do justice to developments since 1992. As a replacement for the old 'blob guide' the Survival Techniques chapter also touches upon a system for predicting company failure, a subject to which I intend to return in more detail in my next book.

The 1980s – the decade of the deal – and the 1990s

Q. How do you become big in the corporate finance business?

A. Start 20 years ago.

Liberalisation and *laissez faire*

Economic growth and Thatcherite deregulation combined with a raging bull market in equities and an easy supply of credit were a recipe for a booming market in houses and take-overs, and that is what the 1980s saw, particularly in the United States and the UK. In the UK, the take-over fires were fanned by a number of factors. Together these created a situation in which the 1980s have come to be known as 'the decade of the deal'. Icons of the age, many of which have since fallen, included the eponymous Donald Trump, who even wrote a book called *The Art of the Deal.*

First among these factors was a Government committed to the freedom of the markets and to financial liberalisation. This saw an end to Exchange Controls, which helped to fuel cross-border investment and take-over activity, and the imposition (for that is effectively what it was) of Big Bang on the cosy cartel which constituted the London Stock Exchange. This in turn led to the disappearance of most traditional stockbroking firms into integrated securities houses complete with expensive corporate finance departments keen to justify their existence. This is an important factor to realise because there is no doubt that many of the deals which grabbed the headlines, particularly towards the end of the 1980s, were hatched in the City's corporate finance departments.

It is no surprise that some of the most spectacular disasters involved the new generation of integrated houses rather than the established mergers and acquisitions players, such as the merchant banks Schroders or Warburgs, and Rowe & Pitman or Cazenove amongst the brokers. There is a saying in the investment world that if you want to be big in the corporate finance business you need to start twenty years ago. What is means is that there is no substitute for connections, judgement and even integrity. But that did not stop the new integrated houses trying. They backed the upstarts of the corporate world with their leveraged bids and grandiose schemes, for the more traditional, i.e. safe, corporate clients were mostly closed to them. So it was that Barclays de Zoete Wedd were advisers to the ill-fated British & Commonwealth, and County NatWest to Tony Berry's Blue Arrow. Probably the single most important word in the corporate finance business is 'No' – when said to a client to explain why his deal will not work and cannot be backed. But is a word which can cost a firm clients since it is one which thrusting entrepreneurs and captains of industry are not accustomed to hearing. Only those with an existing sound corporate list of clients can risk telling a John Gunn that British & Commonwealth should not take over Atlantic Computers, or Tony Berry that they cannot get the institutions to take the shares he needs to issue to buy Manpower. The new integrated houses appeared not to have faith in their corporate client lists. Had someone said the word 'No' they might have saved Messrs Gunn, Berry and their investors a literal fortune.

Hand in hand with the Government's liberalisation of the financial markets was the *laissez faire* attitude to the resulting upsurge in take-over activity, particularly from the mid-1980s. Virtually no one was safe from the rigours of the market. Household names such as Rowntree were gobbled up by the Swiss. Jaguar was driven into American hands and what was left of the British computer hardware industry (ICL and Apricot) was consumed by the Japanese. This trend has revived in the mid 1990s, with Rover being sold to BMW, and most of the UK securities industry and the newly privatised regional electricity companies (RECs) disappearing into often foreign hands.

Through all this upheaval, the Bank of England was relaxed, but stood firm on one issue, which was to protect the clearing banks from anyone who was not "fit and proper" – polite language for anyone who was 1) foreign, or 2) might inject some commercial reality into those most unloved of British institutions. But even the Bank of England could not resist the take-over tide completely and there were plenty of sacrificial lambs amongst the merchant banks as Hill Samuel was swallowed by TSB, Guinness Mahon by the New Zealand-based Equiticorp, and Morgan Grenfell by Deutsche Bank. The fact that Equiticorp quickly went bust and was engaged in a share support operation suggests that the definition of fit and proper could be stretched to include foreigners with improbable finances if they were willing to relieve the Bank of England of a potential problem.

As a result, Hongkong Bank, which had been barred from taking over The Royal Bank of Scotland by the Bank of England in 1981 allegedly because the Bank was concerned about standards of banking supervision in Hong Kong (some rich irony here given the Bank's own experience of matters such as Johnson Matthey Bankers, BCCI and more recently, Barings), was eventually able to gain control of Midland Bank when the recovery plans of Sir Kit McMahon (himself a former Deputy Governor of the Bank of England) were torpedoed by the recession.

Indeed, although the 1990s are shaping up in a remarkably similar fashion to the 1980s given the take-over boom in 1995, they are difference in at least one respect: the waning influence of the Bank of England is protecting its flock from take-over. Apart from Midland, TSB did not last a decade as a quoted company, and ended by falling into the arms of Brian Pitman's Lloyds Bank. Most of the major UK securities houses and merchant bankers have also lost their independence, usually foreign buyers. Smith New Court, the UK's leading equity market maker, is now part of Merrill Lynch. Kleinwort Benson, who kicked off the privatisation boom with the BT sale in 1984, is now owned by Dresdner Bank. Hoare Govett has passed into the hands of ABN AMRO, and Barings was rescued, if that's the right word, by ING. But the greatest surprise of all was that the bear market in bonds in 1994 effectively brought down the flagship of the UK securities industry: Warburgs. It emphasised the fragility of the UK securities industry that its leader could be laid low by one bad year. Warburgs was not only a leader in its own right in corporate finance, but it also included some famous names which it had brought together at Big Bang: Rowe & Pitman the corporate finance brokers; Akroyd & Smithers the jobbers; Mullens the government gilt brokers; plus a controlling interest in the UK's premier fund management house, MAM.

The statistics

Apart from the Bank of England's belated impersonation of King Canute, there was little to stop the take-over tide in the 1980s, and virtually nothing now. The net result was a staggering flow of bids and deals which culminated in the failed record-breaking Hoylake £13.4bn bid for BAT in the summer if 1989. The statistics are:

Table 3.1 Mergers and acquisitions – the 1980s (£bn)											
	1980	1981	1982	1983	1984	1985	1986	1987	1988	1989	1990
UK* M&A value £bn	1.5	1.1	2.2	2.3	5.5	7.1	14.9	15.3	22.1	26.1	7.9
UK equities: total return %	35.0	13.5	28.9	28.8	31.6	20.6	27.5	8.0	11.6	36.0	−9.7
YOY RPI %	15.1	12.0	5.4	5.3	4.6	5.7	3.7	3.7	6.8	7.7	9.3
Net gearing † %	26	23	25	17	21	21	18	17	18	37	
Average Base Rate %	16.3	13.3	11.9	9.8	9.7	12.3	10.9	9.7	10.1	13.8	14.8
Real interest rate %	1.2	1.3	6.5	4.5	5.1	6.6	7.2	6.0	3.3	6.1	5.5

* Source: DTI. Public companies only.
† Combined Balance Sheets of large UK companies.

The DTI series is not the most comprehensive currently available, but it does go back twenty years and it is the most useful from the point of view of long-term trends.

Table 3.2	Mergers and acquisitions – the 1970s (£bn)								
1970	1971	1972	1973	1974	1975	1976	1977	1978	1979
1.1	0.9	2.5	1.3	0.5	0.3	0.4	0.8	1.1	1.7

The previous peak of M&A activity at £2.5bn in 1972 pales into insignificance compared with £26bn in 1989.

Statistics compiled by the magazine *Acquisitions Monthly*, which include private companies, tell the same story of a merger and acquisition boom in the late 1980s. According to them, the 1988 figure for all M&A activity in the UK was £32bn, rising to £52bn in 1989.

Themes

As the tables show, economic growth, the bull market and low interest rates underpinned the huge rise in take-over activity. In addition, it seems that every take-over boom has to have a number of fashionable themes into which companies and institutions can charge herd-like. Even without the benefit of hindsight, many were founded on highly dubious assumptions and were executed more in the heat of the moment than on any prudent assessment of the financial implications.

'One stop' financial shopping

Aside from Big Bang, the liberalisation of financial markets gave rise to the concept of the 'financial supermarket' where the public could purchase everything from mortgages and pensions to home contents insurance and unit trusts. It was this concept that was a major factor in the expansion of British & Commonwealth (B&C) and the rush by insurance companies, building societies and some banks to acquire estate agents in order to produce mortgage and insurance business. The concept was fine on paper, but it ignored one simple and very obvious fact: the clearing banks had been in a position to offer a basket of financial services for years, and had largely failed in their attempts to 'cross-sell' new services to existing customers. Sir Peter Middleton, the Deputy Chairman of Barclays, tells a story which illustrates this problem, about an incident which occurred shortly after he joined Barclays and was touring some branches. He found a group of customers queuing outside a branch to use an auto-teller machine in the rain when the branch's cashier counters were virtually empty. He invited on member of the queue to come inside to use the cashiers. When they got inside the man had cashed his cheque he expressed relief saying "I thought for one terrible moment you were going to try to sell me some life insurance".

The new generation of financial supermarkets fared little better than the clearers had. Apart from the B&C disaster (see Appendix II), the Prudential and Abbey National were forced to do an embarrassing *volte face* and to sell their estate agency chains, virtually giving them away for losses of hundreds of millions of pounds. Hambros, which deployed the cash it raised from the sale of its stake in Hambro Life (Allied Dunbar as it became) into estate agency at close to the top of the market, is still struggling with the loss making Hambro Countrywide.

If it's a growth market, we will make money

Investors have consistently lost money by assuming that if they invest in the equity of companies engaged in a growth market it is logical that they must make money. They should take a leaf from the book of US investors in the 1970s who correctly identified air travel as a growth market and then underperformed the market by investing in airline stocks. How? Because they missed the point that the link between growth in air travel and the profitability of airlines was about to be broken by the intervention of a force called deregulation. More air miles were flown, but at lower and lower fares.

Similarly, UK corporates in the 1980s correctly identified trends such as the demography which was making the current middle-aged generation in the UK the first consistently to inherit property from their parents which would give them free capital to invest. Theories such as this spurred the amazing multiples which were paid for fund management operations, such as Hypobank's acquisition of Foreign & Colonial and Bank in Liechtenstein's bid for GT or NatWest's bid for Gartmore on twenty times earnings. On a grander scale, Lloyds Bank acquired Abbey Life and most of the other acquired or established their own life insurance operations. What they all missed was the extent to which sales of life policies had been dependent not upon inheritance and demographics, but the housing market which sold endowment policies. And when that collapsed in 1990, so did the life market. To compound the pain, there was then the scandal about the mis-selling of personal pensions.

1992 and all that

The preparations for the single European market in 1992 was another reason to hype the take-over game, although this appeared to afflict those investing in the UK more than the other way around. Indeed, corporate UK, still hamstrung by an inability to speak foreign languages, continued to be besotted more by the United States than by the opportunities in its own backyard. This is shown by the following table:

Table 3.3 Spending on corporate acquisitions into and out of the UK				
	1990		1989	
	No.	Value £m	No.	Value £m
UK Domestic	1228	14062	1825	29572
UK into EC (excl. UK)	279	4522	380	3655
UK into Europe (excl. EC)	19	177	30	69
UK into US	167	4998	262	10198
UK into others	69	1326	92	1168
EC (excl. UK) into UK	167	5668	122	5165
Europe (excl UK) into UK	31	436	42	1299
US into UK	47	1171	51	9171
Others into UK	51	6341	38	2025
Source: *Acquisitions Monthly*				

Now that 1992 has passed it is easy to see that it has made very little difference. Nevertheless, investors who suffered from Morgan Grenfell's brief quoted existence will have been grateful for the bid in 1989 from Deutsche Bank at 2.3 times book value. However, they were not as grateful as former investors in Equity & Law and Pearl Assurance. The former was taken over by Compagnie du Midi on 54 earnings, and the latter by AMP (Australian Mutual Provident) on 29 times earnings. Even allowing for the embedded value of the long-term business, both exit multiples were very generous and now look even more so given the recent slowdown in life assurance and pension sales.

And the irony of it all is did 1992 make any difference? None that I can discern, Still it was a good slogan to get a few deals going.

Conglomerates and unbundling

The conglomerates have been nearly as acquisitive as ever during the 1990s. BTR found a new lease of life under Australian Alan Jackson and bid for Hawker Siddeley in 1990. Hanson bought ConsGold and Beazer, swopped gold for forests with Jimmy Goldsmith, bought Quantam Chemical, sold Beazer Homes and US Industries and bought Eastern Electricity. Tomkins out bid Hanson for Rank Hovis McDougall and most recently acquired Gates Rubber in the States.

But the take-over boom of the 1980s reached its high-water mark with a move towards unbundling. Like many of the phrases coined in the 1980s take-over boom, unbundling is an ugly word which sits appropriately alongside other inventions such as the junk bond and greenmail. The phrase can be attributed to Sir James Goldsmith, whose Hoylake consortium including Kerry Packer and Jacob Rothschild planned to unbundle BAT. In the end, BAT partially unbundled itself, selling to Argos and Wiggins Appleton. In fact the practice had been perfected as early as 1986 by Lord Hanson with one of the UK's original mega bids, the take-over of Imperial Group. Or was that asset stripping? It's so easy to get confused.

Unbundling proved to be exportable across the Atlantic where it was akin to taking coals to Newcastle. Indeed, Hanson was adept at unbundling over there as over here, SCM being perhaps the pinnacle of his US achievements. The titanium dioxide interests were retained and the rest of SCM was re-floated. This gave the US market some practice in discovering that things should generally not be bought from Hanson, a lesson which the UK markets has recently relearned with Beazer Homes. Then of course, ICI appeared to offer the greatest prize of all, but eluded Hanson.

But herein lies the catch. Growth through continued acquisition is like a drug. The more successful each deal is, the bigger the next deal has to be to make an impact and continue the pattern of growth. This was the seed of some of the creative accounting practices which came to bedevil corporate UK in the late 1980s. The take-over vehicles not only found that bigger and bigger take-overs were necessary to maintain profits growth, but also found a series of techniques associated with acquisitions and disposals which could be used to boost profits.

The final stage in unbundling for Hanson, king of the acquisitive conglomerates, came when it announced its own split into four businesses since it could no longer add value by acquisition.

MBOs and LBOs

With the exception of the £2bn Isosceles deal for which Warburgs earned in the region of £20m in the summer of 1989, mega bids involving buyouts and buyins by a company's management or others were not a major feature of the UK corporate scene in the 1980s to the same extent that they were in the US, where they culminated in KKR's bid for RJR Nabisco, immortalised in the book *Barbarians at the Gate*. Apart from Isosceles, the three major deals involving householdnames in the UK were Magnet, Lowndes Queensway and Woolworth. Unfortunately, the timing of the first two, at the top of the consumer boom, was to be catastrophic. Both deals were dashed on the rocks of rising interest rates from mid 1988 which led to crippling costs of debt service on the one hand and falling demand for their products on the other. In the end, the banks who advanced the loans for the leverage were left holding the baby. But just to show that the corporate finance market is good at recycling, Magnet has since rejoined the ranks of the stock market by being reversed into Berisford after it was purchased from the long-suffering banks for a song.

The decade was not without some success in the MBO market with the Premier Brands buyout from Cadbury Schweppes standing out in the somewhat safer area of food processing. The Woolworth buyout (originally Paternoster Stores) succeeded where the other retail MBO failed – partly because it happened in an earlier stage of the retail cycle, a conclusion which has been reinforced by the difficulty which Kingfisher (as Woolworth has been rechristened) experienced in 1994/95. Timing in this area of M&A activity, as much as anywhere else, is crucial.

Even a brief résumé of the LBO/MBO market in the 1980s would not be complete without mentioning the relatively small management buyout of the commercial service activities of British & Commonwealth by Bricom in June 1988 for £359m. Although B&C retained a 22.5% interest this was effectively the beginning of the end for the group, because it removed most of the tangible assets from the Balance Sheet, leaving only a highly dubious pile of goodwill relating to the newly acquired financial companies. These proved to be of little support when the Atlantic Computers take-over finally bought the house down. The Bricom buyout was done on an exit PE of 19.6, but there was much hidden value in the various commercial services companies reflecting very conservative accounting policies over the years.

The new owners were quickly able to unlock this value. Over half the acquisition loan was repaid within eighteen months. The 1990 medium-term debt instalment was paid a year early, and in March 1990 the forced sale by B&C of most of its 22.5% stake to other investors was done at a price twice as high as the management buyout. Within a few months the crazy accounting at Atlantic Computers has brought B&C crashing to earth in one of the most dramatic UK corporate failures ever. And, as if to add insult to injury, the debt free Bricom was sold to a Swedish buyer for £338m. It, effectively, was the B&C of the Cayzers. Old money and prudent accounting had survived and prospered despite an initial mountain of debt. The brash financial services conglomerate built with highly rated paper and supported by what proved to be invisible earnings, was strangled almost at birth.

Hence the saying: What is a definition of a recession? A time when money is returned to its rightful owners. The brash financial services conglomerate with its poorly accounted computer leasing subsidiary was not really a store of wealth. It had just borrowed it from the Cayzers, the founders of B&C, who had introduced John Gunn only to find that his strategy was not to their taste. Their money was promptly returned to them when B&C went bust through the guarantee which Barclays Bank had given for the repayment of the preference shares they took when they left (see Appendix II). How suitable an epitaph for the Decade of the Deal.

It will all be different this time

In 1992 the ending of this chapter was called 'And now the hangover'. It went through the litany of shattered companies and reputations that resulted from the take-over boom of the 1980s. But this no longer seems appropriate since a new take-over boom is upon us, marked by the upsurge in activity in 1995:

Table 3.4 UK take-overs 1990–1995						
£bn	1990	1991	1992	1993	1994	1995
UK public companies acquired	10.7	6.2	9.9	3.0	5.1	[No breakdown of data]
UK private companies acquired	6.8	5.9	4.5	5.7	12.5	
UK divestments	10.2	6.0	5.3	8.6	7.2	
	27.7	18.1	19.7	17.3	24.8	67.8

What are the themes of this new take-over boom? The recovery from the recession has been characterised by low growth and low inflation. The net result is that many companies are finding that their automatic ability to increase prices as a method of growing turnover and keeping ahead of rising overheads is gone. The consumer has been fed on a diet of discounting and continuous sales during the recession. Retailers finding themselves squeezed are in turn squeezing their supplies. This is a natural consequence of a low inflationary environment. How else can low inflation be imposed than through price restraint?

In banking, in contrast to the 1980s, the 1990s have seen a dearth of loan demand as the housing boom has ended and corporate UK and Essex Man have both learnt the downside of debt gearing. This has led to the odd combination of a lack of growth in income, as loans are the main generator of interest and non interest income, and burgeoning capital since there is no growth in loan assets to finance. The result of similar conditions in America, i.e. surplus capital and few opportunities to lend, has been a merger mania amongst the regional banks. After all, if you cannot increase profits by growing income, how about cutting costs? Merging banks and cutting out duplicated branches and head office functions is supposedly a route to this, although that ignores research and common-sense which shows that the larger banks are less not more cost efficient. But this has not stopped the US merger mania going beyond the regional banks to encompass the merger of Chemical Bank and Chase Manhattan.

In M&A what happens in America today is the UK's fad of tomorrow. Lloyds has already bid for TSB, and the merger has been hailed by the market as another stroke of genius from Brian Pitman since the new enlarged bank is bound to be more cost efficient. In fact, this was Lloyds' second major acquisition within four months; it had acquired the Cheltenham & Gloucester building society in the summer of 1995. Abbey, the building society which floated in 1989, has bid for the National & Provincial building society, and it would be a brave man, or a foolish fund manager, who would bet that this marks the end of merger mania in the UK's financial sector. Never mind all the research which shows that take-overs rarely deliver value for shareholders, or that larger banks are less cost efficient. In the world of M&A you must never let the facts get in the way of a good story!

Similar pressures have also produced a new wave of take-overs in the pharmaceutical sector in the 1990s. The industry has a good recession, when it proved yet again that spending on healthcare is little affected by economic conditions. But the recovery found it in less good shape. Governments had become alarmed by the inexorable rise of healthcare spending, particularly spending on drugs, as a proportion of GDP, and none more so than in America, the world's biggest healthcare market. This combined with imminent expiry of some key patents which protect the profitability of drugs, most notably on Glaxo's Zantac, the world's best selling drug. The exact response to this likely slowdown in sales growth has varied slightly, but there are common elements with the response of other sectors, such as the banks, in Glaxo's blockbusting bid for Wellcome which was based on the premise of lowering research costs for the combined group. Other responses were more difficult to fathom.

One response to spiralling drug costs in America was the mushrooming of so-called pharmaceutical benefit managers. These organizations managed healthcare programmes to extract the best purchasing deals for drugs and other services. The drug companies' response was to buy them in a wave of take-overs in 1994–95. How a pharmaceutical benefit manager would fit within a drugs company with whom it was meant to play hard ball in price negotiations was to say the least unclear. It seems a bit like putting the fox in charge of the hencoop, a fact which may not be entirely beyond the grasp of the Federal Trade Commission. But it was clearer than the logic behind the prices paid. SmithKline Beecham paid for $2.3bn for Diversified Pharmaceutical Services, a company with operating profits of $39.9m and assets of just $60m. But according to analysts, despite the exit multiple of 88 times historic earnings, the acquisition did not dilute earnings. What is even more amazing is that analysts actually copied this statement down and sent it out to clients under the guise of research.

But events in another sector which has been a take-over theme for the 1990s make those in banking and pharmaceuticals seem almost sane. I refer of course to media. If you have a company into which you can fit the words 'multi media', the world is your oyster. There has been a scramble for terrestrial TV stations in the UK, and groups such as Pearson have decided that they are no longer conglomerates with the *Financial Times*, Lazards, Madame Tussauds, Wedgewood, etc. but media groups, which they went on to demonstrate by buying Thames TV, Grundy Television (makers of the *Neighbours* soap opera), and Mindscape, a maker of cartridge games for computers and CD-ROM. Dorling Kindersley, the publisher of illustrated books, had a period of glory when some of its books were published on CD-ROM by Microsoft, the dominant force in software under Bill Gates, which also took a stake in the company. A soaring share price and M&A deals were the reward for any company which could claim the slightest association with the Internet. Never mind that most investors and other ordinary mortals had no acquaintance with the Internet of multimedia at all, and even those who were involved struggled to find a way to profit from it. It was a growth market, so these deals were bound to make money. Where have I heard that before?

Even the supposedly boring privatised utilities enjoyed their own take-over boom, especially the RECs, which were bid for by US utilities, water companies, conglomerates, other RECs and power generators. No one seemed to stop in the middle of this feeding frenzy to reflect that the take-overs were occurring in the run-up to a General Election which seemed very likely to return a Labour Government – which might have a marked effect on the profitability of these utilities. But then that's a take-over boom for you.

Source: Smith, T. (1996) *Accounting for Growth: Stripping the Camouflage from Company Accounts*, London, Century Business, 2nd Edn, Ch. 1–3, pp. 1–23

1.3 Shareholder value

Peter Clarke

What exactly is Shareholder Value? How do we achieve it? Should we report it in the financial statements? What are companies doing about it? Professor Peter Clarke offers some answers.

Introduction

The term 'value' has gained increasing usage in the business literature in recent years. For example, business managers and management accountants will make reference to the value chain and value-added activities, auditors are familiar with the concept of value for money and the preparation of value-added statements was recommended but rejected some years ago. It seems that we have come a long way since Oscar Wilde remarked that a cynic is one who knows "the price of everything, and the value of nothing".

This short article is about shareholder value. This term began to feature prominently in the 1980s and was, in many respects, popularised by Alfred Rappaport in his book *Creating Shareholder Value* (Free Press, 1986). He reiterated the proposition that the appropriate goal for commercial organizations is to maximise shareholder value via dividends and increases in the market price of the company's shares. While this principle is widely accepted – corporate mission statements often proclaim this to be the primary responsibility of management – there is substantially less agreement about how this is to be accomplished and whether shareholder value metrics should be reported in the annual financial statements. Some interesting material has recently been published in this regard and is covered in this article structured around the following questions:

- What is shareholder value?
- How do we achieve it?
- Should we report shareholder value in the financial statements?
- What are companies doing about it?

What is the shareholder value?

The fundamental assumption of shareholder value is that a business is worth the net present value of its future cash flows over a defined timeframe, discounted by the cost of capital appropriate for the business. This assumption is well supported by modern corporate finance theory. What is important is that a company adhering to shareholder value principles concentrates on cash flow rather than profits. Secondly, it always puts the shareholder first in terms of company goals. This seems to conflict with conventional wisdom that customer satisfaction/loyalty is the most important goal. However, a company that fails to deliver value to customers is acting against the long-term interests of shareholders. The corollary would be to offer products and services without regard to profit: customers would be delighted but shareholder value would be destroyed.

How do we achieve it?

The corporate goal of creating shareholder value is determined by seven value drivers, highlighted in Table 1. These seven macro level factors vary between industries but the assumption is that improvement in any of these value drivers leads to an increase in shareholder value. These value drivers can be classified into three categories – operating, investing and financing that represent the major functions of any business.

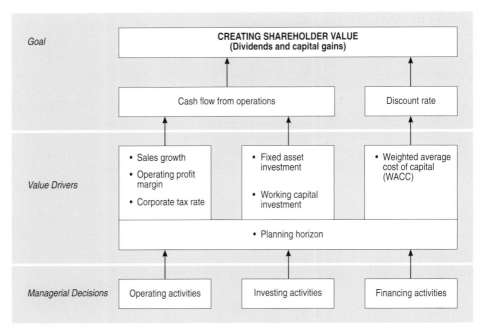

Table 1   *Creating shareholder value*

Operating decisions such as product mix, pricing, advertising and levels of customer service are impounded primarily in three value drivers – sales, growth, operating profit margins and corporate tax rates. The first two drive the amount of cash coming in to the business whereas the corporate tax rate drives the amount of cash going out. Investment decisions are defined in terms of fixed asset and working capital investment. In addition to these, there is the weighted average cost of capital (WACC) which is the rate of return demanded by investors – in relation to both debt and equity – based on the risk associated with the business and its capital structure. For management, the insight offered by a 'value' focus is that the use of capital is not 'free'. Rather, it is invested in the expectation of earning a return and this required return defines the company's cost of capital. The company creates shareholder value only if it generates returns in excess of its cost of capital. Therefore, the seventh value driver is the planning horizon over which a particular strategy can be expected to deliver competitive advantage. For example, a company may depend on a product that is expected to hold its place in the market for, say, five years. After that, a new product will be needed. So, planning or competitive advantage period is five years.

The major benefit of using shareholder value comes from linking management decisions to value through the planning horizon and the key value drivers. For example, in some companies, sales growth will destroy value because of the additional working capital requirements and fixed asset investment. Value can also be destroyed through acquisition. In fact, value can be destroyed even though reported accounting profits and EPS are positive.

Thus far we have simply re-iterated a commonly held view that creating shareholder value has been central to the objective of firms since the foundation of corporate enterprises. As a perspective, it has become enshrined in principles of corporate financial reporting. We have also stressed the importance of cash flow in terms of valuing firms. What is new, in terms of emphasis, is the realisation that management only creates value. Management can only create value for shareholders if the company consistently, over the long term, generates a return on capital, which is greater than its cost. Management creates value by developing a strategy that builds on the business's competitive advantage. In addition, management is required to implement that strategy, to recognise and manage the risk inherent in that strategy and to identify future sources of potential advantage, including market trends.

Should we report shareholder value in the financial statements?

Why should companies report on shareholder value creation? One simple answer is that financial statements are supposed to be useful to investors (and other users) and an important characteristic of useful information is its long-term, future orientation. Currently, financial statements, prepared in accordance with accounting standards, are focussed on past events and historical financial performance and provide little information about future-orientated matters. Relying only on financial statements for decision-making purposes has been likened to driving a car using the rear view mirror!

Admittedly, companies now produce an Operating and Financial Review (OFR), but surveys show that companies have been slow to respond to the challenge of providing forward-looking information. Yet, investor surveys confirm both investors' desire for more forward-looking information in a company's annual report and the importance to their investment decisions of strategic matters and key drivers of future performance. Thus, if management is entrusted with the responsibility of creating value through their strategic initiatives then, surely, they should report on their progress. However, there are crude assumptions and extreme computational difficulties associated with the shareholder value calculations. In such circumstances, it is reasonable to argue that investors (actual and potential) look for softer, more qualitative evidence that management has set its sights on creating shareholder value. In other words, management should report more transparently to investors on the chosen strategy and the key indicators of successful implementation of that strategy. Since this information may be unaudited, management credibility will become a crucial factor.

This is the thrust of the 1999 discussion paper by the ICAEW. [1] Their proposals are intended to provide a framework for explaining a company's strategy, and the progress that the company is making towards achieving that strategy. The proposals create an important link between external financial reporting and the internal management practices and could be described as forming part of an integrated performance measurement system. Interestingly, the proposals relate to all companies whose shareholders are remote from management. The recommended disclosures help to address shareholder value considerations. They relate both to the company as a whole and, to each significant business activity of the company, in respect to:

- Strategy
- Markets and competitive positioning
- Key performance indicators and 'value' based measures of performance

I have no doubt in suggesting that the recommended levels of disclosure will come as a surprise to many managers of Irish companies. I would venture to suggest that some managers may be unable to comply with these recommendations simply because they have not been required to think in such dimensions! If managers choose to disclose a new measure, it is important to articulate why that measure is important and why it affects 'value'. The outlined proposals are viewed as providing a practical framework for the introduction of a more forward looking perspective into annual financial reports. Many of the recommendations are based on practices observed in other countries.

Conclusion

This article has focussed on shareholder value that may be described as a perspective which acknowledges that management is primarily responsible to shareholders. Shareholder value is created only by management and so, it is reasonable to suggest that management should report both why their strategies are expected to lead to the creation of value over the long term and their own view of actual performance. Such information will benefit individual shareholders and firms, and facilitate the Stock Exchange in allocating scarce capital resources. Really, there is nothing radically new about these proposals which may, in time, be referred to as strategic financial reporting. They are attempting to address the criticism: "when I get my accounting report I am either happy or sad, but rarely wiser"!

Source: *Accountancy Ireland*, October 2000, Vol. 32, No. 5, pp. 10–11

[1] *Inside Out: Reporting on Shareholder Value*. Financial Reporting Committee, ICAEW, 1999.

1.4 Performance auditing

Charles Rush

The internal auditor has traditionally shunned publicity and seldom discusses professional matters outside of the internal audit community.[1]

Some years ago I was in Laos where I met a mad man. This person insisted on calling everyone only by their job title, so I was 'auditor'. On first meeting, he told me that he killed auditors, but later, in a kinder mood, he explained this applied only to 'internal' auditors. Fortunately I then worked for an external audit organization and I eventually returned home safely, reflecting on the differing perceptions that the consumers of audit service have of audit providers – what they expect of them, what they really receive and what they should receive.

For instance, few can have escaped noticing the monotonous regularity with which seemingly healthy corporations suddenly fail – BCCI, Polly Peck, Maxwell Communications, Barings – to name some recent examples in the UK alone. Nor is the public sector exempt from financial shock waves, such as the Western Isles – population about 32,000 – Council's £23m investments with BCCI – a large chunk of it being borrowed money reinvested with the bank; or Hammersmith and Fulham Council's little eight-year foray into the SWOPS market to the tune of a staggering £6 billion, subsequently described by a senior judge as 'akin to gambling'.[2] None the less, many audit consumers still believe that there is a higher echelon of auditors that can normally be relied upon to protect them from such events, their 'objectivity' – the ability to make unbiased factual judgements – being assured by their 'independence' of the organization being audited. Hence their pronouncements, in the form of audit certificates, should be reliable.

Far fewer people may be aware that there is also another form of auditing – internal auditing. But, among those who do know of its existence, there persists a strong view that, by virtue of it being *internal* – that is, part of, and paid directly by, the organization – it can never attain the same credibility as the independent, external auditor in terms of objectivity. Its recommendations are accordingly viewed in a lower light.

After several years operating in both roles, I have concluded that this view is fallacious, resulting from a misreading of the world as it really is. This article explains what auditing really is and can do and the limitations imposed on it. In the second part, I will argue that audit providers and audit consumers need to realign their expectations by demanding a more holistic audit emphasis, encompassing a wider range of stakeholder interests – that is, auditors need to accept responsibility for the credibility of all performance information, thereby becoming true 'performance auditors'.

External or internal – what is the difference?

Accounts do not necessarily have to be completely correct and therefore, when you reach your opinion, judgements have to be made on the materiality of any discrepancies.[3]

Primarily, external and internal auditors have different roles. The external auditor's prime task is to perform 'financial audits'; that is, to carry out sufficient checks, in accordance with professionally agreed standards. In the UK these are known as SASs – Statements of Auditing Standards, laid down by a joint committee of the six main professional accounting associations. [4] These standards are designed to enable the auditor to 'certify' the accounts – that is, pronounce on their validity. Such pronouncements are required by various national regulations; for example, in the UK the Companies Act 1985 and in the European Union to an extent by the Fourth Directive on company law issued on 25 July 1978, which attempted to harmonize international accounting practice.

In performing this task, external auditors avoid saying the accounts are 'correct'. In fact, for over 40 years UK accountancy bodies have been required to show only that the accounts of companies show 'a true and fair view'. The UK accounting bodies were instrumental in promoting the adoption of this concept throughout the European Union through the Fourth Directive. Yet a study by researchers at Loughborough University in 1990/91[5], of the interpretation placed on the concept by the 'technical audit partners of the "top thirty" accountancy firms in the UK', found that those interviewed had a distaste for the concept mainly because 'of the spurious precision implied by the word "true" and the ambiguity of the formula.' In fact, some of the individual replies were even more illuminating; for example, one practitioner stated 'I have never quite satisfactorily worked out in my own mind what "true and fair" means'. Consumers of external audit service beware.

The role of the internal auditor is different and is unlike the mainstream accountancy profession which, as research by Simmonds and Azières[6] among others has shown, is notable for its disharmony in the practices it applies (in spite of the Fourth Directive). Internal audit, on the other hand, has achieved very considerable and real international agreement over its role and practices. The Institute of Internal Auditors UK (IIA UK) lays down its 'Standards and Guidelines for the Professional Practice of Internal Auditing'.[7] This is a detailed operational guide which includes a Code of Ethics. But there is nothing especially national about these guidelines. For instance, they are almost word-for-word the same as those issued by the USA-based Institute of Internal Audit Incorporated (IIA Incorp.), which directly sets internal auditing standards for the whole of North America and Mexico. Furthermore, the rapidly developing European Confederation of Institutes of Internal Auditing (ECIIA) – comprising 17 nationally based bodies, including the IIA UK – is working with the IIA Incorp. and the Latin American Federation Latino America de Auditores Internos towards creating a global alignment of national institutes, all broadly working to the same compatible standards.[8] As Jacques Renard states of L'Audit Interne, 'Celle-ci est, en effet, organisée au plan international, elle obéit à des règles communes qu'elle s'est imposée.'[9]

Already internal auditors show remarkable agreement in defining their prime role. To the IIA UK:

> *The objective of internal auditing is to assist members of the organization, including those in management and the board, in the effective discharge of their responsibilities. To this end, internal auditing furnishes them with analysis, appraisals, recommendations, counsel and information concerning activities reviewed. The objective includes promoting effective control at reasonable cost.*[7]

Organizations' managers should observe that two consequences flow from this Standard:

1 It does not set any limit on whom internal audit should assist within the organization – any manager can benefit from the internal auditor's services. By implication, therefore, the internal auditor should not exist solely to promote the financial director's influence (as is often thought to be the case).

2 The work of the internal auditor should be directed towards improving managers' 'effectiveness'. There are possibly as many internal auditors as audit consumers who fail to appreciate the impact that this statement should have on auditing. It means that, in order to comment on effectiveness, the audit should begin at the strategic level, with an understanding of what really is required of the operation being audited. The issue of the adequacy of control and value for money (VFM) are therefore, or should be, subservient considerations, examined in the context of strategy. Thus the requirement to 'think strategically' is fundamental to internal auditing.

The roles of external and internal auditors should therefore be very different. The former have the very narrow responsibility for evaluating one set of performance data – that is, the organization's financial statements – and pronouncing on their validity, in accordance with a concept that is, at best, questionable. True, external auditors do other work, and all external auditing firms now provide vast and profitable consultancy services, but the basis for their existence is still certifying financial data. Internal auditors by comparison are concerned with effectiveness, anywhere in the organization, and their ability to succeed hinges on their ability to measure a performance dimension in any area throughout their respective organizations. Thus internal auditors' ability to give value could be significant. In practice, few internal auditors or consumers of audit services view internal audit in this way – why?

This partly relates to the question of perception, already referred to above, which in turn flows from the link made between independence and objectivity and the consequent inferior status given to internal auditing. Unquestionably, external auditors work for bodies that are legally distinct – separate – from the body being audited and internal auditors, normally, do not. But does this inevitably mean that 'objectivity' – unbiased factual judgement – is the exclusive preserve of one and not the other? People who maintain that this is the case may, perhaps, be confusing two quite different concepts of independence.

One relates to independence in the physical sense that one person's body is independent of another's, or two countries have physical borders and laws and international agreements that establish their legal independence of each other. However, what is really being defined here is 'separateness'. Conceptually, this is distinct from 'objectivity' as defined above, and the mere existence of a recognized separation between two bodies, countries, or corporations does not in any way guarantee one will be objective about the other. Conversely, and perhaps more significantly, it does not rule out the possibility that a body can be objective about itself. Hence, independence used in the sense of separateness should not be regarded as synonymous with objectivity.

In effect, the link between independence and objectivity that is actually sought from auditors relates to the concept of independence of mind – the right to make judgements based upon a person's own observations, free of any influence. In this pure, detached sense it is unlikely to be found anywhere in organizational relationships because issues such as culture, economics, organizational and political interests intervene and affect relationships as much between as they do within organizations. For this reason, neither the external nor the internal auditor can claim objectivity as their exclusive preserve.

External audit firms have corporate 'independence'; that is, they are legally separate from the audited organization. But they are none the less commenting on the other organization and they are very conscious of the need to do this without upsetting these 'clients'. Officially, external auditors are reporting to the shareholders and are appointed by them, but in practice this is on the recommendation of the senior management who is the real 'client'. External auditor relations with clients is a delicate area: a great deal is involved, both for the firms and for the individual auditors performing audits. First, there is the audit fee – no firm wants to lose it and no audit team wants to be associated with losing it! Then there is need for the auditor to maintain co-operation. It is perhaps not often realized just how essential this is to external auditors. Remember that they are operating in a strange administrative framework and on someone else's territory – they don't even know where the toilet is – and without co-operation the audit takes longer and this costs more. The audit firms may not be refunded for a longer visit and, even worse, they could lose lucrative consultancy work. These are real everyday pressures exerted on external audit firms and on individual external auditors which undermine the independent state of mind so associated with objectivity.

One of the prime concerns of the 'Cadbury'[10] Committee was external auditor and client relationships. This Committee was set up by the City of London in response to the series of unexpected corporate failures in the UK. It reported in 1992 with a recommended voluntary 'Code of Best Practice' for regulating registered UK companies' financial affairs. For instance, it wants fees paid to the external auditor for non-audit work to be 'fully disclosed'. It is too early to say what impact this report will actually have. But, if the subsequent shock collapse of the oldest merchant bank in the City of London – Barings plc (with its last audited accounts showing it to be financially profitable and a very safe bet) – is anything to go by, it has not solved the problem of the inability of external auditors to pronounce objectively on the real health of an organization.

Conversely, consider the reality of the position of the internal auditor. The Chief Internal Auditor and staff are usually on the payroll. Is this good or bad in terms of a potentially independent mind? To start with, it certainly means they are not worrying about getting the fee paid and a contract renewed for the next year. In truth, I suspect that most internal auditors' level of uncertainty is much lower than that of most external auditors. Heads of internal audit are not dismissed lightly. Not only do they have some protection under the contracts of employment legislation but, probably far more importantly, they know a lot of very intimate details about the organization and that knowledge is a strong bargaining counter. Again this does not guarantee an independent mind, but it certainly does not rule it out either. Finally, internal auditors have a long-term commitment to the organization – they want their organization to succeed and they are going to be around when their recommendations come to fruition!

If internal auditors are employed by an organization that wants unbiased reporting, the internal auditor can provide it. Of course, they are subject to a variety of pressures that might influence them and for that reason they could never claim to make 'objective' judgements in the purest sense – but frankly the same is true of the external auditor.

It is therefore argued that audit consumers should shift their focus away from the issue of audit independence and should instead take a much harder look at the real value they obtain from the auditing profession. In these terms, the external auditors provide very little purely by virtue of being 'external'; their prime value is in the credence they give to the reports of past financial performance. As such they are, and should more properly be called, 'financial auditors', who provide limited comfort to some external stakeholders. They give value because this comfort factor eases relations with those external stakeholders who would not be happy without it.

However, as writers such as Eccles[11] have identified, many more stakeholders, both internal and external, require a far broader range of performance information to help them make decisions for the future. The prime concern of these stakeholders is organizational effectiveness; that is, how well equipped are they to survive and give their customers the service or products required? But the information required to provide this broader picture also needs to be credible and reliable; that is, it needs to be audited. Therefore, the question that audit consumers should be asking is could internal audit – with its stated role of promoting effective control throughout the organization – assume a wider role of 'performance auditor' for all performance information? The good news is that it could – based on a technique called *systems based auditing* (SBA). Developed mostly by internal auditors for assessing control of financial systems, and now regarded as best practice for auditing such systems, this approach could easily be transferred to assessing control over any other system in an organization, with only minor adaptations. The bad news is that there is little sign of it being given this wider role.

Therefore, the second part of this article examines what SBA is, considers what has prevented internal auditors from using it in a wider organizational context and looks at what it could do for organizations if that were to change.

Systems based auditing

> *The auditor will learn one of the difficult lessons of life – how to get on with the other chap and appreciate his point of view.*[12]
> (Extract from notes for internal audit staff in the Home Counties, 1950s)

Other than the need for interpersonal skills expressed above (albeit in the words of a different age), much has changed in internal audit practice since the 1950s. However, the impact has been diminished by the length of time it has taken the internal audit profession to adopt the new techniques involved.

The underlying principle is very simple – it is better to prevent errors happening in the first place than try to spot them after they have occurred. This amazingly obvious statement led to the development of SBA.

The term 'systems' used by auditors is very much related to hard system thinking whereby a system is viewed as an interconnected sequence of inputs, processes and outputs, the boundaries being readily definable. Such systems can be administrative and financial activities – for example, paying invoices (i.e. a payables system) – or the provision of services – for instance, assessing and granting or refusing planning consent – or any other distinct process – for example, the manufacture of a chocolate bar. SBA assumes that, where such systems are appropriately controlled with the right mix of measures to prevent, detect and correct malfunctions, the desired outputs will result.

The methodology is applied in two stages. The first relates to identifying which systems are to be audited and when. This stage is a continuous cycle of activities (see Figure 1).

The first activity – identifying main systems – simply refers to systems that are essential to achieving the organization's financial goals (note 'financial goals' – more to follow on this below). The second activity is perhaps the most difficult in what is otherwise a logical sequence. It involves categorizing the systems into their ascending order of risk, using a series of risk factors relevant to each organization's context. For instance, Figure 1 shows the factors that might be considered relevant to a public authority. The second stage – implementing individual 'planned' audits, which is activity 4 on Figure 1 – takes the form of the logic path for each audit shown in Figure 2.

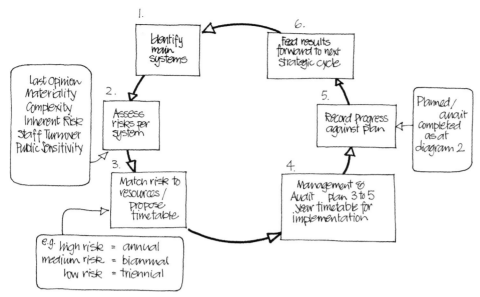

Figure 1 *Audit strategic cycle*

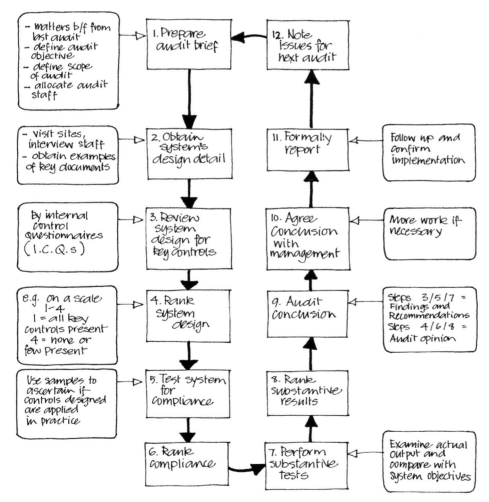

Figure 2 *Systems audit logic path*

The logic path's core consists first of steps 2 and 3 – obtaining and reviewing a description of the system. This involves recording the prime processes, documents and people making up the system, understanding their interrelationship (often flow-charts are used for this) and then noting the control mechanisms designed to prevent processes deviating from their intended path. The description is then compared with a standard control model for a similar system. (This is called an Internal Control Questionnaire because it is framed in the form of a series of questions about whether there is control at 'key' stages in the system.) For example, a payables system would be expected to contain a check that the supplier's invoice 'matched' the order and the delivery note before it was paid. Deficiencies in control are then noted for discussion with the people involved. (This is because an apparent deficiency may be a result of a weakness in the system's design, or a consequence of a peculiarity of its operational context, hence the need to 'talk it through' with managers and staff, before reporting.)

Secondly, steps 5 and 7, known jointly as 'testing the system', distinguish audit from other review tools such as evaluation and monitoring. The latter primarily rely on reports and witness statements, sometimes backed by observations which may or may not be representative; whereas audit pronouncements should be backed by firsthand observations that are representative (this usually involves sampling in such a way that an unbiased overview is obtained). In this way the auditor takes responsibility for his or her opinion. Compliance testing – usually based on samples – examines whether, in practice, controls designed to operate in a certain way actually do function as intended – the reality being that things do not always happen as senior managers think they do. For instance, a computer system containing commercially sensitive information may have been designed to report unauthorized attempts to access it – for example, by people using the wrong password – which then need to be investigated. In practice, a report is produced, properly labelled 'access violations', but the auditor discovers that it is not sent to anyone because there are two managers involved who cannot agree whose job it is to review it.

Substantive testing is the auditor's final safeguard. Here the system itself is ignored; instead, the auditor takes a representative sample of final outputs from the system which are examined, with two objectives. First, where system design and compliance testing have indicated weaknesses, substantive testing allows the auditor to gauge the impact this has on the end results. Sometimes there is a knock-on effect that causes problems all the way down the line, with severe consequences not appreciated at the point where the weakness arises. In other cases, a significant weakness is compensated for by diligent staff taking corrective action. Secondly, the examination of the design and compliance testing has its limitations. Recording what should happen and testing whether it does leaves the possibility that something has been missed from the equation altogether. For example, it is not unknown for an informal set of processes to be in place and running alongside the formal ones. Frequently this is because changes have been made without the participation of staff, who continue to operate part of the old system because they believe 'it works'; but problems can arise where it is now outside of the new control mechanisms. It is important that the auditor spots these changes and takes them into account. This is achieved by examining actual outputs which are checked back to the processes that have actually produced them.

SBA therefore provides managers with an overview of the adequacy of their control, thereby ensuring that systems act as intended. By 'as intended' auditors would normally mean conformity with the organization's stated objectives and policies, whether such objectives and policies are best for the organization or not. However, the fact of highlighting system weaknesses and/or output failure can cause an organization to re-examine the underlying objectives and policies themselves. For instance, the auditor may find that reserves stocks for a particular market are excessively high. This may cause the organization to reconsider the strategic need to be in that market in the first place. Thus SBA is a relatively sophisticated example of single loop control which can fit comfortably within a double-loop control framework.

Within the audit profession SBA does have its critics. Bold initiatives are said to be in the offing to replace it. For instance, the IIA (UK) has reported one such 'new approach' called 'Control and Risk Self Assessment'. [13] Essentially it provides a framework in which audit consumers conduct their own assessment of risk and, by such means as brainstorming (with the auditor acting as facilitator), find their own control solutions. Actually, whilst these initiatives cause some people in the auditing profession to think about what they are doing – which is in itself desirable – they do not diminish the underlying SBA principle that prevention is better than cure. What they are really advocating is greater participation by the people operating the system, at each stage in the SBA process, which the structure in Figures 1 and 2 can accommodate where auditors and consumers want it. The real problem with SBA lies not with the technique itself, but with its narrow application by auditors to systems in one functional area – finance. But this is not the fault of the technique.

Those readers who are familiar with quality or environment management may have already observed a similarity between SBA and the processes recommended for 'auditing' quality and environmental assurance systems. For instance, the basic environmental audit 'steps' recommended by the International Chamber of Commerce[14] are almost identical to the standard systems approach shown in Figure 2. In effect SBA, which had its origins in traditional auditing fields long before terms such as 'environmental audit' were first articulated, is a generic auditing approach. It can be applied to any performance system and this is being done; but rarely by the traditional audit discipline. Given that they have the skills, why have traditional audit providers shunned this market, leaving it to other non-audit professionals to fill the vacuum?

The answer is linked to an even more fundamental mystery: why, given that SBA is such a logical approach to auditing, with its emphasis on prevention rather than cure, did it take so long to be accepted? My research has not found any one person who could claim to be the original SBA guru. Certainly, however, articles appearing in auditing journals in the USA and UK during the 1950s began to refer to the need to change audit's emphasis. For example, an article in the June 1957 edition of the US-based *The Internal Auditor* by the Assistant Comptroller of Colgate-Palmolive (with the thought-provoking title 'Managers want more help') stated that 'The purpose of reviewing procedures is not to discover what employee made what mistake or judgement error, but rather to improve managerial control and prevent deficiencies in the future'.[15] Yet in 1977 Professor Bristow of Strathclyde University was reporting that there is only a 'gradual broadening' of the auditing role so that 'mistakes can be avoided from the start instead of identified retrospectively'.[16] And in 1986 a survey of 400 local authority internal audits in England and Wales found that 'systems audit work is also extremely variable in quality, with very little really good work being performed' and that some sections 'are convinced of its benefits, though not yet prepared to apply it'.[17] Why then has the auditing profession been so reluctant to respond to managers' needs, in spite of the need for it being recognized by some auditors for at least 30 or 40 years? Again, real world reality provides the explanation.

Ours is not to reason why – the accountants do that!

> *Internal Auditing is a well established and progressive department, and is involved in every aspect of the group's activities.*[18]
> (Advert for Deputy Head of Internal Audit, Barings plc, 26 February 1995 – five days later the company ceased trading in its own right, forever.)

There are two major explanations for internal audit's slow response to the needs of audit consumers – its history and its continuing functional subservience.

Internal auditing had an inauspicious beginning, starting in the accounting departments of old, where clerks sat in rows making manual entries in ledgers and journals. Sometimes they made mistakes. Occasionally, some involved in handling cash stole it. To counter this, other clerks – called internal auditors because they were 'internal' to the department – formed more rows and laboriously checked the work of the first set of clerks.

Although it was devoid of initiative and deadly boring, none the less it provided the certain pleasure that some people derive from catching others out. It also had two significant advantages. First, by adding up the mistakes found, the chief auditor had a ready means of justifying the work. Secondly, since money permeates the whole business one way or another, the audit department often found itself checking actions taken in departments other than finance, where similar mistakes were found. However, these were mistakes on someone else's territory, and the chief auditor's boss – the chief accountant – was not slow in appreciating the advantage this gave in the internal politicking that goes on everywhere. Thus, although it made good organizational sense to move towards preventing mistakes instead of finding them after the event, chief auditors and chief accountants did not always see it as serving their interests.

Furthermore, the tendency within organizations as they age for bureaucratic hierarchies to form and become fixed into accepted structures did not encourage finance or non-finance managers to question the auditor's place within the finance department. Thus, internal auditing has suffered from a natural desire for comforting cultural certainties that perpetuate territorial sovereignty over certain professions.

Hence, internal audit has found it very difficult to break out of its early mould. Often, albeit reluctantly, the logic of new techniques such as SBA has been recognized and applied; but chief accountants have mostly managed to retain a firm functional grip on the audit department – by maintaining the myth that auditing and finance are synonymous. The reality is quite different. As quality and the environment have shown, other functional performance information requires auditing and auditing techniques are readily transferable to these areas. Likewise, internal auditors can, and should, be drawn from a variety of functional backgrounds and belong to none. If this were more often the case a different vision of the audit role could emerge, with finance receiving the audit attention merited by its strategic role, and better balanced organizations being encouraged.

Performance auditing – a change of attitude not technique

Take the customers' perspective and ask 'Do I care?' If the answer is no, the work adds no value.[19]

There are many different theories of the life cycle of organizations; for instance, Alfred Chandler found that organizations move through three stages of development – unit, functional and multidivisional with the transition often both delayed and painful.[20] In practice, I believe that public or private organizations can be placed in, or between, one of four positions: (1) new, where they are in the process of deciding their culture and practices; (2) settled, where their processes and culture are established and routine, with relative mid-term certainty – for example, the classic bureaucratic public sector operation; (3) unsettled, where the organization is no longer new but is in a constant state of uncertainty – for example, organizations at the forefront of market or political fashion, such as education; (4) reorganizing, where a complete rethink is taking place. Organizations never stand completely still; even settled organizations eventually move on. Sometimes they will alternate between settled and unsettled phases and sometimes organizations, in any position, will fail and become non-survivors. The reason they change position or fail is in response to pressures from within and without, and whilst pressures are changing all the time they never cease. Figure 3 – not dissimilar to many management models – portrays this vividly.

Figure 3 distinguishes those organizations that adapt, reposition themselves and survive from the non-survivors. An organization's prospects of being a survivor are greatly enhanced by the possession and use of performance information that is applicable to the position they are in. Here I am referring to performance information that accords with Eccles' thinking;[11] that is, a package of measures that matches a strategy designed to ensure the organization continues around the cycle. All of this information – which, depending on the strategy, might include financial, marketing, environment, human resource management (especially on training and retraining programmes) – needs to be reliable, complete and timely.

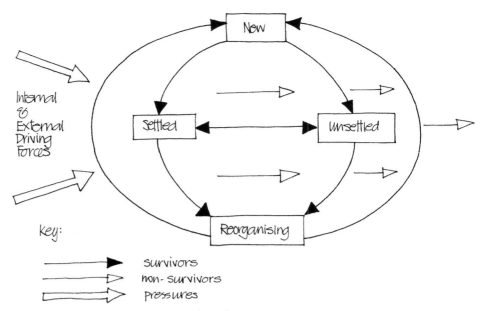

Figure 3   *The organizational cycle*

If it is not, the organization will be deceiving itself and, sooner or later, will find itself, unexpectedly and unceremoniously, forced out of the cycle.

Ensuring that the whole package meets these criteria is the role of the performance auditor. The performance auditor would apply techniques such as SBA and its derivatives (for instance, the moves to inject greater staff participation into the auditing process) to auditing *all* performance systems that are critical to the organization's success. Furthermore, by adopting a holistic approach from the system identification stage (see Figure 1), the performance auditor would be in a position to comment not merely on individual performance systems but, at the strategic level, on the suitability of the package as a whole. For example, a strategy that was dependent on a successful retraining programme would have an assessment in the form of an independent audit on its implementation and on the relative resources put into training. Such an audit approach would create a better balance within organizations and provide a rational basis for controlling change.

The performance auditor would give value by intervening, making the difference between information that gets it right rather than gets it wrong and by ensuring that appropriate weight is given to the performance systems that are significant to the contemporary needs of the organization. That would be an audit service worth paying for.

Notes

1   Courtemanche, G. (1986) *The New Internal Auditing,* John Wiley & Sons, p. 1.

2   Lord Justice Templeman (1991) House of Lords, Hazell v. Council of the London Borough of Hammersmith and Fulham.

3 National Audit Office (circa 1986) *A Guide to Certification Audit in the National Audit Office*, p. 80.

4 Statements of Auditing Standards (SAS) are laid down by a joint committee (the Auditing Practices Board) of the six main professional accounting associations in the UK – called collectively the CCAB (Consultative Committee of Accountancy Bodies).

5 Higson, A. and Blake, J. (1992) *The True and Fair View Concept – A Formula for International Disharmony: some empirica! evidence* Loughborough University Business School. Presented at the Audit Conference, University of Central England in Birmingham, 16 September.

6 Simmonds, A. and Azières, O. (1995) 'Accounting for Europe – success by 2000 AD?', in Holloway, J. *et al.* (eds) *Performance Measurement and Evaluation,* The Open University/Sage Publications, pp. 217–247. Originally published by Touche Ross Europe, 1989.

7 The Institute of Internal Auditors UK (1994*) Standards and Guidelines for the Professional Practice of Internal Auditing*, p. 3.

8 Garitte, J.-P. (1995) 'Get to know the ECIIA', *IIA Today* – the Journal of The Institute of Internal Auditors Inc. USA January/February.

9 Renard, J. (1994) 'Théorie et pratique de l'audit interne', *Les Éditions d'Organisation,* p. 81.

10 Committee on the Financial Aspects of Corporate Governance (1992) *Report of the Committee on the Financial Aspects of Corporate Governance,* Gee and Co. Ltd, p. 55.

11 Eccles, R.G. (1995) 'The performance measurement manifesto', in Holloway, J. *et al.* (eds) *Performance Measurement and Evaluation,* The Open University/Sage Publications, pp. 5–14. Originally published in *Harvard Business Review,* January–February 1991.

12 Chief Internal Auditor of the Home Counties (1950s) *Notes for Guidance of Internal Audit Staff* p. 40.

13 Oxley, T. (1993) 'Introducing a new approach to control and risk management', *Internal Auditing* (Journal of the Institute of Internal Auditors – UK), April and May.

14 International Chamber of Commerce (1989) *Environmental Auditing,* first published in English, June, pp. 14–15.

15 Kenyon, M.A. (1957) 'Managers want more help', *The Internal Auditor* (Journal of the Institute of Auditors), June, p. 52.

16 Bristow, R.J. (1978) 'The changing role of the internal auditor', *Internal Auditing,* November. Presented at the National Conference of the Institute of Internal Auditors – UK, September 1978, Stratford-on-Avon.

17 Audit Commission (1986) *Survey of Internal Audit in Local Government in England and Wales – A Report prepared by CIPFA and the Audit Commission*, p. 4.

18 *The Sunday Times* (1995) 'Appointments', 26 February, pp. 6–16.

19 Hammer, M. and Champey, J. (1993) *Re-engineering the Organization,* p. 125.

20 Chandler, A.D. (1989), quoted in Stoner, J.A.F., and Freeman, R.E. (eds) *Management,* 4th edition, pp. 227–228, Prentice Hall, Englewood Cliffs, NJ.

Source: *B889 Performance Measurement and Evaluation*, Supplementary Readings, Milton Keynes, Open University Business School, Edn 4.1, 1997, pp. 109–120

1.5 The use of ratios to forecast company failure

J. M. Samuels, F. M. Wilkes and R. E. Brayshaw

Financial ratios are an indication of the financial strength of a company. However, they are only an indication; they do not prove anything. They are a trigger mechanism: if a ratio is out of the ordinary, questions need to be asked. There might be perfectly satisfactory explanations for the particular size of the ratio, but the ratio does need an explanation.

A number of researchers have attempted to forecast company failure based on the levels of the company's financial ratios. One distinguished writer on this topic in the USA is Altman. In one of his studies he examined characteristics of a number of companies that became liquidation over a period, and the characteristics of a sample of companies that remained solvent over the period. [Please note that, in the UK, the terminology is that a firm or company goes into liquidation whereas, in the US, a firm is said to go bankrupt.] He used a statistical technique known as multiple discriminant analysis in an attempt to differentiate between the two groups. Initially he considered 22 potentially helpful variables (ratios), but from this list five variables were selected 'as doing the best overall job together in the prediction of corporate liquidation'. Of these five, the liquidity variable which was found to be more useful for discrimination purposes than either the current ratio or the liquidity ratio was:

$$\frac{\text{working capital}}{\text{total assets}}$$

where working capital equals current assets minus current liabilities. The other four ratios were:

$$\frac{\text{retained earnings}}{\text{total assets}}$$

$$\frac{\text{earnings before interest and taxes}}{\text{total assets}}$$

$$\frac{\text{market equity value}}{\text{book value of total debts}}$$

$$\frac{\text{sales}}{\text{total assets}}$$

The discriminant ratio model proved to have some success, with correct predictions in 94% of the liquidation cases. Altman claims that 'investigation of the individual ratio movements prior to liquidation corroborated the model's findings that liquidation can be accurately predicted up to two years prior to actual failure'.

The one ratio that made the largest contribution to differentiating between the two groups was the current profitability ratio: earnings to total assets. In fact there was no evidence of liquidation in companies earning profits. This may seem an undramatic observation, but it does underline the importance of considering liquidity ratios in a dynamic context. A company may have a current liquidity problem, but if it is profitable the flow of funds should be able to remedy the liquidity position. This explains the importance of considering the ratios in conjunction with the current flow of funds.

Altman found that the Z score model was a good forecaster of failure two years prior to liquidation. The model was able to predict with 95% accuracy one year prior to liquidation and with 72% accuracy two years prior to liquidation. The accuracy diminished substantially as the lead time to liquidation extended beyond two years. The model was not used to examine its usefulness in predicting the failure of small firms.

Following Altman, numerous studies attempted to improve and extend the liquidation classification process. One was a zeta model, which is claimed to be quite accurate at predicting liquidation up to five years prior to failure. This model used seven financial variables, covering return on assets, stability of earnings, interest cover, cumulative profitability, the current ratio, size and a gearing ratio. The most significant variable was found to be cumulative profitability, which is measured by the ratio of retained earnings to total assets.

There are two types of error that can arise with such predictions. One is that the model will fail to identify a company that is in financial distress, and the other is that the model will identify a company as having a high probability of failure when in fact it is sound.

It should be appreciated that all accounting numbers can do is indicate something has gone wrong within a company. The cause of the financial distress is usually bad management, and the mistakes have already been made before that fact is revealed in the financial accounts. Those investing in companies and those making credit available may well have left it too late if they wait for the publication of the annual accounts in order to assess the company's strengths and weaknesses. Analysts should look for the symptoms of failure.

A number of other researchers have used a similar technique to that of Altman. Multiple discriminant analysis attempts to find the combination of variables which best discriminates between two or more groups. This involves attributing weights to each variable such that the distribution of scores obtained for each group have the least overlap. In the application of this technique in the financial distress area one group consists of those companies that went into liquidation during the period of study, and the other group consists of those companies that survived. The variables used to discriminate are of course the financial ratios. Having determined the relative importance of each ratio, these weights can then be used to predict the chance of failure for any company.

Research in the UK in this area has been led by Taffler. In his 1982 paper he reports that as a result of testing the usefulness of 50 ratios the five most significant from a discrimination point of view were:

$$\frac{\text{earnings before interest and tax}}{\text{total assets}}$$

$$\frac{\text{total liabilities}}{\text{net capital employed}}$$

$$\frac{\text{quick assets}}{\text{total assets}}$$

$$\frac{\text{working capital}}{\text{net worth}}$$

$$\frac{\text{cost of sales}}{\text{stock}}$$

The first two of these five ratios were found to be the most significant. The first ratio is a measure of the flow of funds into the business resulting from the company's own operations. It was also found to be important in Altman's study. The second ratio shows the outside claims on the resources of the business. The fifth ratio indicates stock turnover.

The Bank of England has looked at the potential of this technique. Their model did not show results that were particularly encouraging. The Bank concluded that 'careful analysis of accounts over a long period together with scrutiny of other published information is likely to provide the best, indeed the only basis for any adequate assessment by an outsider of the financial position of a company'.

The discriminant approach is still used, however, to indicate companies at financial risk. A financial data service is available in which figures are produced that indicate the chance of a particular company failing.

There are many theoretical problems with this type of statistical analysis. There are also problems with the accounting data. Nevertheless, the results of these studies and other similar types of work are used by financial analysts and bankers.

Many of the studies have only used financial ratios. A few studies used mixed models (with some cash flow variables and some financial ratios). The cash flow ratio most often used in such studies is cash flow to total debt. Other cash flow statistics used in the prediction of failure are cash to sales, cash to current liabilities and cash flow from operations.

It is hoped that there is more to the use of this approach than just 'self-fulfilling prophesies'. If bankers and analysts use the technique and believe in it, then any company that ranks badly as a result of the analysis might well find its funds cut off. As a result the company will fail and the technique will have been said to have worked!

Conclusions

A very popular way of analysing the performance of a business is through the use of financial ratio analysis. Impressions formed on the basis of this analysis can affect decisions as to whether to supply the business with goods on credit, whether bank loans will be made available, whether a company will be given a stock market listing, and whether or not to buy the company's shares.

Accounting by its nature has to be an inexact subject. It is necessary to make many assumptions in preparing a set of financial accounts. All attempts to value a company must be estimated, whether based on measuring asset values or based on expected future cash flows. Nevertheless, those operating in the stock market must make decisions every day on what they believe should be the value of a company's shares.

Source: Samuels, J. M., Wilkes, F. M. and Brayshaw, R. E. (1995) *Management of Company Finance*, London, Chapman & Hall, 6th Edn, pp. 63–65

2.1 When is a budget not a budget? A "cultural revolution" for budgets?

Brian Rutherford

A number of large multinationals have recently been reported as having "scrapped" their budgets. Budgets are said to be a major barrier – sometimes, indeed, *the* major barrier – to success in a knowledge-based economy. Even new approaches such as activity-based budgeting must be swept aside if enterprise is to thrive. Managers must be liberated from the straitjacket of annual beancounting rituals and empowered, with a mission to "beat the competition not the budget".

So what does "managing without a budget" involve? One company that abandoned the annual budget process in 1994 is reported to have replaced it with:

- monthly, three month ahead, forecasts;
- monthly out-turn reports with key performance indicators;
- two year ahead rolling forecasts, updated three monthly;
- four year strategic plans, revised annually; and
- 10 year strategic plans, revised annually.

So, no bureaucratic straitjacket there, then.

On the face of it, abolishing the budget seems to be a matter of ensuring that no document that has financial captions down the left hand side and periods across the top also has the word "budget" anywhere on the page – call it a forecast, a target, a forward look or a summary of the strategic plan and, hey presto, you've abolished the budget! But there is more to it than that. The burden imposed by a system is not necessarily easily inferred from a bare description of it and the sort of elaborate information flows prescribed in the list given in the previous paragraph may well be easier to manage and impose less of a burden than the simple but demanding regime of the traditional budget.

Furthermore it may well be that the new system provides better information for planning, motivating, steering the business, evaluating performance and beating the competition. It has to be admitted that there is a lot wrong with budgeting, as traditionally conducted, from all these angles and it doesn't take much imagination to suggest improvements – though it can take a great deal of imagination to envision what the new system will look like and a great deal of courage to make the leap from "tried and understood" to "new and innovative".

The question I want to raise is whether the rhetoric of budgetary "slash and burn" is either appropriate to what is going on or helpful.

The problems that arise in setting an annual plan and expecting it to unfold without hesitation or deviation over the ensuing 12 months have been known and understood for decades. Early responses to these problems included the concept of flexing the budget and it is, indeed, depressing how little even this modest innovation has been taken up in practice – no doubt partly for fear that it will be used as an excuse for underperformance. Other responses included rolling budgets, updated quarterly or monthly. The motivational side of budgeting, including the need to set "stretch" budgets, has also been much discussed.

Although the extent to which these developments have been implemented is limited, this does not demonstrate that budgeting needs to be abolished – only that more imagination, energy and courage needs to go into developing and designing planning and control systems to suit the 2000s and beyond. We already know a good deal about what goes wrong (and what goes right) in budgeting and it is unnecessary – and expensive – to abandon all this knowledge in pursuit of a "cultural revolution".

Knowledge-based economy

For example, it is often suggested that the new cultural revolution is needed because the world of manufacturing has been replaced by a knowledge-based economy. Many knowledge-based resources, such as intellectual property, brands and loyal customer bases, do lie outside traditional accounting measurement systems, but there is no reason why they have to. Knowledge is a resource and we have a great deal of experience in using budgets to manage resources (and some businesses, such as drug companies, have been in knowledge-based sectors and used budgets for decades). We should first examine carefully what lessons we can learn from this accumulated experience before we abandon it too lightly.

Again, a "budget-less" management system advocated in some quarters is the Handelsbanken model, which employs relative targets: each branch of the bank competes with all other branches via league tables drawn up on the basis of key performance targets. It is claimed that, under this system, the targets are always up-to-date, always tightening, and strongly motivating because of peer pressure. The first problem with the Handelsbanken model is that the system requires that the organization is composed of large numbers of homogeneous units – true of banks and, perhaps, retail stores, but of almost no other type of organization. Using external comparators introduces all the problems of bench-marking – widely recognised as an extremely useful source of insights but not necessarily of targets. Further, even in an organization that is composed of the right sort of units, the system can work only if the organizational culture is appropriate. If not, branch managers will quickly realise what production line staff have known for many years, that by co-operative action and social sanctions, a group can control the targets their managers believe they are setting with enormous cunning. We need to remind ourselves of the Hawthorne experiments of 1927–1932, a massive set of studies of behavioural modification that demonstrated, among many other things, how groups control "rate-busting". A simple example here of a lesson learnt and understood three-quarters of a century ago that might all too easily be forgotten in the new cultural revolution.

Incidentally, internal competition under the Handelsbanken model might be thought to be divisive and likely to lead to turf wars, charges often levelled against traditional budgeting by the advocates of its overthrow. Proponents of the Handelsbanken model argue, however, that it is free of these vices because a strongly supportive culture encourages co-operation and the spread of best practice. But if culture can overcome the potential divisiveness of internal competition, surely it can overcome the same problem under traditional budgeting?

Fortunately, much of the apparently revolutionary and abolitionist literature and practice is in fact evolutionary, developing better solutions from what has gone before. The range of quasi-budgets replacing the "one true budget" in the example given above demonstrates this.

There are advantages to the presentation of the changes as a cultural revolution. Some are real: it emphasises management commitment to the new way of working and provides an opportunity to throw out more of the baggage that goes with systems than perhaps could be accomplished with an overtly evolutionary approach. Some are less real: it no doubt impresses the shareholders, but for how long?

A potentially serious consequence of the revolutionary façade, viewed from the point of view of the accounting profession as a whole, is that it can discourage companies, particularly small and medium-sized enterprises, from reaping the advantages to be gained from developing a more sophisticated approach to budgeting because they believe they must throw out everything and start again – a far more expensive, and risky, move than is really necessary. Thus, whole areas of the economy are cut off from a potentially useful development.

The last slash and burn management fad to dominate the headlines was down-sizing. We now know that this was a potentially dangerous cult that could easily lead to "corporate anorexia". Strategic financial managers need to be careful that the same mistake is not made with the budget.

Source: *Accounting & Business*, September 2000, pp. 14–15

2.2 Getting the most from budgeting

Alison Kennedy and David Dugdale

Alison Kennedy and David Dugdale look at some of the reasons for dissatisfaction and frustration with the budgeting process and suggest ways in which they might be reduced, if not eliminated.

While some proposed management accounting techniques seem to be little used in practice, this cannot be said of budgeting. Surveys have shown that 99% of all companies in Europe operate formal budgeting systems. Most management accountants spend a considerable amount of time preparing, revising and monitoring budgets and most organizations have clear and well proven budgeting routines. However, many participants express dissatisfaction and frustration with the budgeting process. This short article will look at the reasons for some of the frustrations and will suggest ways in which they might be reduced, if not eliminated.

The budgeting process results in the creation of a set of interlocking budgets, which project financial results for a future period (often a year). A budget can be defined as 'the quantitative expression of a plan of action and an aid to co-ordination and implementation of the plan'. In theory the preparation of budgets should proceed logically through a series of steps:

1 Establish the corporate mission and objectives.

2 Set environmental assumptions; hence determine the limiting factor – usually sales.

3 Set the budget for the function constrained by the limiting factor.

4 Set other budgets, co-ordinating with the limiting factor and the corporate objectives.

5 Synthesise all budgets to produce a master budget.

6 Review the master budget in the light of the corporate objectives.

7 Accept the master budget or, if the master budget does not meet corporate objectives, go back to 2 and repeat the process until the master budget is acceptable.

8 Monitor actual results against budgeted results and report variances.

9 As a result of variances, either (i) take corrective action to eliminate variances or (ii) revise the master and subsidiary budgets to accommodate the variance.

This description suggests a simple, readily understandable, ordered process. Why, then, does it lead to such frustration? We believe that the problems of budgeting primarily arise because budgeting serves a variety of purposes. Six key functions of budgets have been identified:

- a system of authorisation;

- a means of forecasting and planning;

- a channel of communication and co-ordination;

- a motivational device;
- a means of evaluation and control; and
- a source of information for decision-making.

The academic literature recognises that the conflicts associated with these multiple functions of budgets cannot easily be resolved. In the following sections we consider how budgets might be designed to accomplish particular functions, how this leads to conflict and finally, the lessons that can be drawn for practice.

Budgeting for motivation

There is a wealth of empirical evidence that supports the proposition that budget targets have an impact on results – the budget is not just a neutral planning and reporting tool but is itself a determinant of final outcomes. Studies have shown that 'tight but achievable' budgets normally lead to the best results, i.e. performance superior to that which would have been attained with other targets, or no targets at all. Thus, if the budget is to be used as a motivational device leading to good results, then 'tight but attainable' budgets should be set.

Such budgets are, typically, of 'medium difficulty'. Consider the consequences if budgets are much tighter or slacker than this. The evidence shows that, if an easy budget is set, managers are likely to bring their aspirations into line with the budget – achieving less than if there had been no budget at all! Budgets cannot be used to motivate good performance if easy targets are set. Very difficult budgets are also usually associated with inferior performance, presumably because budget holders perceive the budget to be unrealistic and are therefore not motivated by it.

However, the evidence on difficult budgets is not clear cut. For example, in his classic study, Stedry[1] found that the actual performance associated with a very difficult budget was dependent on the point in the budgeting process at which the budget holder's own personal goal, or 'aspiration level' was set. Where aspiration levels were set prior to receiving a difficult budget actual performance was very poor – lower even that the performance associated with an easy budget or no budget at all. However, when aspiration levels were set after receiving the budget then, in Stedry's study, the very best performance was associated with this difficult budget. This result suggests that setting difficult budgets is a high-risk strategy. It is associated with both the best and the worst possible outcomes, the dividing line depending on the point at which the budget holders decide on their own personal goals.

These results suggest that, if the budgeting process can be organised so that aspiration levels are determined after the budget has been set, difficult budgets might achieve the best results. The manner in which budgets are set (whether imposed or via a participative process) is likely to affect both the level of personal aspirations and when they are set – thus impacting on actual performance.

A word of caution is necessary before it is concluded that difficult budgets may, under certain conditions, lead to better performance than that obtained when 'tight but achievable' targets are set. Stedry's experiments were not carried out in real business settings and therefore their validity in such settings is not proven. Later studies (which did not consider when aspiration levels were set) indicate that difficult budgets tend to lead to a reduction in both aspiration levels and performance. Perhaps if aspiration levels can be carefully managed there are circumstances where difficult targets will elicit the best response. However, on the basis of available evidence, it is not recommended that very difficult budgets are set if the most is to be gained from budgeting in terms of both motivation and actual performance.

Budgets for planning

When stretching budgets, with significantly less than a 50% chance of being achieved, are aggregated to produce a master budget, the master budget will have a very low probability of being achieved. The precise probability depends on the probability distributions of the component budgets but, given realistic assumptions about these distributions, a probability of less than 0.1 of attaining the master budget is likely. As discussed above, stretch budgets are appropriate to motivate good performance. However, to organise a company around a plan with such a low chance of attainment is clearly inappropriate. An appropriate master budget for planning would be a realistic one, with the actual outcome having a high probability of being close to the budgeted outcome. However, if individual targets are reduced to make the aggregate budget more realistic then the motivational benefits of the individual budgets will be lost.

It has been suggested that two budgets should be constructed – a realistic one for forecasting and planning and a more optimistic one for motivation. In practice this is rarely, if ever, done, possibly because the pain and misunderstanding that one budget can generate is sufficient for most organizations! Many accountants, though, will be familiar with the 'bottom drawer' syndrome – the second budget that no one but the finance director is supposed to know about. Typically, this relatively unsophisticated budget is based on a more conservative assumption than the 'real' budget, and helps the finance director to ensure that plans are realistic. However, while its content may be private its existence is often an open secret and may further add to the anxiety often associated with the budgeting process.

A possible solution to this conflict may be to set budget holders personal targets, which are more challenging than the budget. However, the motivational impact of such targets will be crucially dependent on whether the budget holder can be persuaded that these goals, and not the budget, represent the 'real' target. This in turn will be dependent on the emphasis given to the attainment of each set of targets in the organization's evaluation procedures, i.e. on the accounting style adopted (this is discussed briefly in the following section). The accountant can be influential in the design of the evaluation procedures and also in communicating why the two goals cannot be incorporated into the same system.

Budgeting for control and evaluation

We have seen that budgets of medium difficulty are associated with the best actual performance. Where the probability of meeting or exceeding the budget is around 0.3 the budget holder faces a stretching challenge. Such a budget is difficult, but not impossible, to achieve. As noted above, empirical evidence suggests that such stretching budgets produce excellent results, despite the fact that the results will, on average, fall short of the budget target. This has implications for the way in which budget variances are regarded. Adverse variances are the norm when stretch targets are set. If such variances are used to evaluate the budget holder, placing him or her in a position of failure, then a number of behavioural consequences might be anticipated and this has been an important field for research.

The evidence suggests that the manner in which accounting information is reported, and the consequences which follow from such reports, is an important determinant of the success of the budgeting process. Early researchers confirmed that budgeting style did influence attitudes towards both the budgeting process and actual performance. Unfortunately, the nature of the response to the reporting style was not predictable from study to study and therefore this research did not lead to any specific prescriptions for improved practice.

Later researchers focused on both the form of reporting and the environment in which reporting took place. By looking at these factors simultaneously, it has been possible to draw some general conclusions. For example, when there is a high level of environmental uncertainty, a fact of life for increasing numbers of businesses a 'non accounting' style appears to be most effective. With this style accounting data has only a small part to play in evaluating individual performance and budget adherence is not directly linked to rewards or punishment. An uncertain environment means that a manager's influence on actual outcomes is limited and the attempt to adhere rigidly to predetermined financial targets becomes inappropriate. If such adherence is required it is likely to lead to dysfunctional behaviour by the budget holder. Such behaviour ranges from the creation of excessive budgetary slack (requesting expense budgets far beyond what is needed and being ultra conservative in setting revenue budgets) to falsification of accounting data.

On the other hand, if budget holders have both a high degree of control over budget outcomes and a high degree of independence, then heavy reliance on financial reports, termed a "budget constrained style' does not appear to have negative consequences despite rewards and punishment being associated directly with budget adherence. This evidence suggests that care must be taken to adapt the reporting style to the circumstances of the budget holder if the most is to be gained from budgeting.

The budgeting process: participation or imposed budgets?

As noted above, Stedry's empirical evidence reported that, with difficult budgets, performance is improved if individuals set their own aspiration levels after, rather than before, the budget is finalised. It might seem that participation in the budgeting process would ensure that minds remain open throughout the procedure, eventually giving budget holders 'ownership' of their budgets and leading to improved final results. However, while it might be politically correct to extol the virtues of participation, the empirical evidence to support its value in the budgeting area is mixed. For example, many studies have shown that the personality of the participants in the budgetary process is a significant influence on whether participation leads to improved performance. Much evidence supports the view that authoritarian people are unaffected by participative approaches while high participation is effective for individuals with a high need for independence and low authoritarianism score. It may be possible to take this into account when deciding on the amount of participation that is appropriate for a particular budget holder, although this requires a high level of knowledge of the individuals involved.

The empirical findings relating to the impact of environmental uncertainty on the efficacy of participation may have more general applicability. For example, a study by Mia[2] found that the level of participation should be commensurate with the level of job difficulty. This study showed that participation was effective when both job difficulty and participation were high but that high participation was ineffective when job difficulty was low. These findings accord with both common sense and experience. Many people resent having their time taken in discussing issues which are not contentious, but are insulted if their voice is not heard when they face real problems. When a job is easy an imposed budget may be readily accepted, but this is highly unlikely to be the case in a difficult and uncertain environment. These findings suggested that the level of participation required to get the most from budgeting should be adjusted to the circumstances of the budget holder's environment, which is perhaps easier to determine than the budget holder's psychological profile.

Lessons for practice

It has not been possible in this short article to consider all the functions of budgeting listed earlier. However, our consideration of budgeting theory and our experience of budgeting practice lead us to two observations, which may be of interest to those involved in the budgeting process.

First, we suggest that managers should give careful thought to the particular objectives that they are trying to achieve in budgeting. As it is difficult to achieve all the objectives of budgeting simultaneously care must be taken to ensure that the process achieves the objective deemed to be most important.

For example, if the company is in real difficulties then the most important business objective would be survival and the paramount budget objective would be to set a realistic plan to see the company through the coming year.

An imposed, cost-cutting budget might achieve this overriding objective. However, as noted earlier, the targets set should not be so harsh as to be viewed as impossible or the budget may actually make matters worse. On the other hand, an expanding company may want to ensure that managers are motivated to grasp opportunities while they are available.

Such a company might emphasise the communication, co-ordination and motivational aspects of budgeting while downplaying the planning, authorising and evaluative aspects.

Our second observation is that, once managers are aware of the potential difficulties in budgeting they can take action to minimise the impact of the difficulties. For example, the alternatives 'top down' and 'bottom up' budgeting are often set out as mutually exclusive alternatives. 'Top down' may be effective in forecasting and planning but, as shown above, is likely to be ineffective as a motivational device in many circumstances. 'Bottom up', on the other hand, might aid communication and co-ordination but at the expense of control. However, it is possible to involve budget holders in the development of their budgets while still setting out fairly closely defined limits within which they are expected to operate. This avoids the 'wish list' syndrome where managers initially produce a set of budget requests which is greatly in excess of anything they expect to receive, because they expect to be cut back in subsequent rounds of budget negotiation.

The best results in budgeting will be achieved when a complex mix of factors is taken into account: the personalities of the participants, the type of budget being set – expense or revenue – the degree of uncertainty present and the approach to performance reporting. To incorporate all these factors successfully, often whilst operating within the procedures of the budget manual, requires a high level of sensitivity and excellent communication skills amongst accountants.

As we have seen there has been a long tradition of research into the behavioural consequences of budgeting that should inform practice. However, it is often the technical advances in budgeting theory that are emphasised. For example, in the 1970s zero-base budgeting was introduced – emphasising the planning and authorising aspects of budgets. And in the 1990s activity-based budgeting has been suggested – emphasising a rational and participative approach. These ideas are undoubtedly valuable. Nevertheless, getting the most from budgeting will always require both sound technical knowledge and sensitivity to the likely behavioural consequences of budgeting.

Our analysis and suggestions here hardly amount to 'rocket science'. However, many companies prepare budgets and generations of managers and management accountants seem doomed to learn the lessons of their predecessors the hard way. We believe that careful analysis of what needs to be achieved and how the budget process can help, together with some common sense attention to the details of budgeting can make the process more useful and less painful.

1   Stedry, A.C., *Budget Control and Cost Behaviour*. Prentice Hall, 1960

2   Mia, L, 'The impact of participation in budgeting and job difficulty on managerial performance and work motivation: a research note', *Accounting, Organizations and Society,* 14(4), 1989, pp. 347–57

Source: *Management Accounting*, February 1999, Vol. 77, No. 2, pp. 22–24

2.3 Using the balanced scorecard as a strategic management system

Robert S. Kaplan and David P. Norton

Building a scorecard can help managers link today's actions with tomorrow's goals.

Using the Balanced Scorecard as a Strategic Management System

by Robert S. Kaplan and David P. Norton

As companies around the world transform themselves for competition that is based on information, their ability to exploit intangible assets has become far more decisive than their ability to invest in and manage physical assets. Several years ago, in recognition of this change, we introduced a concept we called the *balanced scorecard.* The balanced scorecard supplemented traditional financial measures with criteria that measured performance from three additional perspectives – those of customers, internal business processes, and learning and growth. (See the chart "Translating Vision and Strategy: Four Perspectives.") It therefore enabled companies to track financial results while simultaneously monitoring progress in building the capabilities and acquiring the intangible assets they would need for future growth. The scorecard wasn't a replacement for financial measures; it was their complement.

Recently, we have seen some companies move beyond our early vision for the scorecard to discover its value as the cornerstone of a new strategic management system. Used this way, the scorecard addresses a serious deficiency in traditional management systems: their inability to link a company's long-term strategy with its short-term actions.

Most companies' operational and management control systems are built around financial measures and targets, which bear little relation to the company's progress in achieving long-term strategic objectives. Thus the emphasis most companies place on short-term financial measures leaves a gap between the development of a strategy and its implementation.

Managers using the balanced scorecard do not have to rely on short-term financial measures as the sole indicators of the company's performance. The scorecard lets them introduce four new management processes that, separately and in combination, contribute to linking long-term strategic objectives with short-term actions. (See the chart "Managing Strategy: Four Processes.")

The first new process – *translating the vision* – helps managers build a consensus around the organization's vision and strategy. Despite the best intentions of those at the top, lofty statements about becoming "best in class," "the number one supplier,"

Robert S. Kaplan is the Arthur Lowes Dickinson Professor of Accounting at the Harvard Business School in Boston, Massachusetts. David P. Norton is the founder and president of Renaissance Solutions, a consulting firm in Lincoln, Massachusetts. They are the authors of "The Balanced Scorecard – Measures That Drive Performance" (HBR January-February 1992) and "Putting the Balanced Scorecard to Work" (HBR September-October 1993). Kaplan and Norton have also written a book on the balanced scorecard to be published in September 1996 by the Harvard Business School Press.

HARVARD BUSINESS REVIEW   January-February 1996

BALANCED SCORECARD

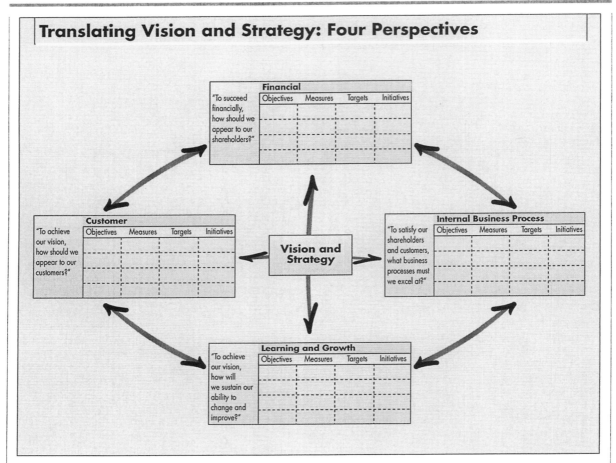

Translating Vision and Strategy: Four Perspectives

Financial
"To succeed financially, how should we appear to our shareholders?"
Objectives | Measures | Targets | Initiatives

Customer
"To achieve our vision, how should we appear to our customers?"
Objectives | Measures | Targets | Initiatives

Vision and Strategy

Internal Business Process
"To satisfy our shareholders and customers, what business processes must we excel at?"
Objectives | Measures | Targets | Initiatives

Learning and Growth
"To achieve our vision, how will we sustain our ability to change and improve?"
Objectives | Measures | Targets | Initiatives

or an "empowered organization" don't translate easily into operational terms that provide useful guides to action at the local level. For people to act on the words in vision and strategy statements, those statements must be expressed as an integrated set of objectives and measures, agreed upon by all senior executives, that describe the long-term drivers of success.

The second process – *communicating and linking* – lets managers communicate their strategy up

Lofty vision and strategy statements don't translate easily into action at the local level.

and down the organization and link it to departmental and individual objectives. Traditionally, departments are evaluated by their financial perfor-

mance, and individual incentives are tied to short-term financial goals. The scorecard gives managers a way of ensuring that all levels of the organization understand the long-term strategy and that both departmental and individual objectives are aligned with it.

The third process – *business planning* – enables companies to integrate their business and financial plans. Almost all organizations today are implementing a variety of change programs, each with its own champions, gurus, and consultants, and each competing for senior executives' time, energy, and resources. Managers find it difficult to integrate those diverse initiatives to achieve their strategic goals–a situation that leads to frequent disappointments with the programs' results. But when managers use the ambitious goals set for balanced scorecard measures as the basis for allocating resources and setting priorities, they can undertake and coordinate

76   HARVARD BUSINESS REVIEW   January-February 1996

only those initiatives that move them toward their long-term strategic objectives.

The fourth process – *feedback and learning* – gives companies the capacity for what we call strategic learning. Existing feedback and review processes focus on whether the company, its departments, or its individual employees have met their budgeted financial goals. With the balanced scorecard at the center of its management systems, a company can monitor short-term results from the three additional perspectives – customers, internal business processes, and learning and growth – and evaluate strategy in the light of recent performance. The scorecard thus enables companies to modify strategies to reflect real-time learning.

None of the more than 100 organizations that we have studied or with which we have worked implemented their first balanced scorecard with the intention of developing a new strategic management system. But in each one, the senior executives discovered that the scorecard supplied a framework and thus a focus for many critical management processes: departmental and individual goal setting, business planning, capital allocations, strategic initiatives, and feedback and learning. Previously, those processes were uncoordinated and often directed at short-term operational goals. By building the scorecard, the senior executives started a process of change that has gone well beyond the original idea of simply broadening the company's performance measures.

For example, one insurance company – let's call it National Insurance – developed its first balanced scorecard to create a new vision for itself as an underwriting specialist. But once National started to use it, the scorecard allowed the CEO and the senior management team not only to introduce a new strategy for the organization but also to overhaul the company's management system. The CEO subsequently told employees in a letter addressed to the whole organization that National would thenceforth use the balanced scorecard and the philosophy that it represented to manage the business.

National built its new strategic management system step-by-step over 30 months, with each step representing an incremental im-

provement. (See the chart "How One Company Built a Strategic Management System.") The iterative sequence of actions enabled the company to reconsider each of the four new management processes two or three times before the system stabilized and became an established part of National's overall management system. Thus the CEO was able to transform the company so that everyone could focus on achieving long-term strategic objectives – something that no purely financial framework could do.

Translating the Vision

The CEO of an engineering construction company, after working with his senior management team for several months to develop a mission statement, got a phone call from a project manager in the field. "I want you to know," the distraught manager said, "that I believe in the mission statement. I want to act in accordance with the mission statement. I'm here with my customer. What am I supposed to do?"

The mission statement, like those of many other organizations, had declared an intention to "use high-quality employees to provide services that surpass customers' needs." But the project manager in the field with his employees and his customer

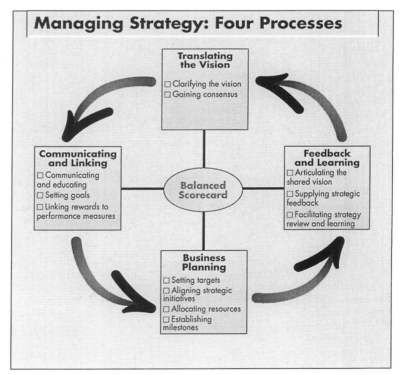

Managing Strategy: Four Processes

Translating the Vision
- ☐ Clarifying the vision
- ☐ Gaining consensus

Communicating and Linking
- ☐ Communicating and educating
- ☐ Setting goals
- ☐ Linking rewards to performance measures

Balanced Scorecard

Feedback and Learning
- ☐ Articulating the shared vision
- ☐ Supplying strategic feedback
- ☐ Facilitating strategy review and learning

Business Planning
- ☐ Setting targets
- ☐ Aligning strategic initiatives
- ☐ Allocating resources
- ☐ Establishing milestones

How One Company Built a Strategic Management System...

2A *Communicate to Middle Managers:* The top three layers of management (100 people) are brought together to learn about and discuss the new strategy. The balanced scorecard is the communication vehicle. *(months 4 - 5)*

2B *Develop Business Unit Scorecards:* Using the corporate scorecard as a template, each business unit translates its strategy into its own scorecard. *(months 6 - 9)*

5 *Refine the Vision:* The review of business unit scorecards identifies several cross-business issues not initially included in the corporate strategy. The corporate scorecard is updated. *(month 12)*

Time Frame *(in months)*

0	1	2	3	4	5	6	7	8	9	10	11	12

Actions:

1 *Clarify the Vision:* Ten members of a newly formed executive team work together for three months. A balanced scorecard is developed to translate a generic vision into a strategy that is understood and can be communicated. The process helps build consensus and commitment to the strategy.

3A *Eliminate Nonstrategic Investments:* The corporate scorecard, by clarifying strategic priorities, identifies many active programs that are not contributing to the strategy. *(month 6)*

3B *Launch Corporate Change Programs:* The corporate scorecard identifies the need for cross-business change programs. They are launched while the business units prepare their scorecards. *(month 6)*

4 *Review Business Unit Scorecards:* The CEO and the executive team review the individual business units' scorecards. The review permits the CEO to participate knowledgeably in shaping business unit strategy. *(months 9 - 11)*

did not know how to translate those words into the appropriate actions. The phone call convinced the CEO that a large gap existed between the mission statement and employees' knowledge of how their day-to-day actions could contribute to realizing the company's vision.

Metro Bank (not its real name), the result of a merger of two competitors, encountered a similar

Building a scorecard enables a company to link its financial budgets with its strategic goals.

gap while building its balanced scorecard. The senior executive group thought it had reached agreement on the new organization's overall strategy: "to provide superior service to targeted customers." Research had revealed five basic market segments among existing and potential customers, each with different needs. While formulating the measures for the customer-perspective portion of their balanced scorecard, however, it became apparent that although the 25 senior executives agreed on the words of the strategy, each one had a different definition of *superior service* and a different image of the *targeted customers.*

The exercise of developing operational measures for the four perspectives on the bank's scorecard forced the 25 executives to clarify the meaning of the strategy statement. Ultimately, they agreed to stimulate revenue growth through new products and services and also agreed on the three most desirable customer segments. They developed scorecard measures for the specific products and services that should be delivered to customers in the targeted segments as well as for the relationship the bank should build with customers in each segment. The scorecard also highlighted gaps in employees' skills and in information systems that the bank would have to close in order to deliver the selected value propositions to the targeted customers. Thus, creating a

78

7 *Update Long-Range Plan and Budget:* Five-year goals are established for each measure. The investments required to meet those goals are identified and funded. The first year of the five-year plan becomes the annual budget. *(months 15 - 17)*

9 *Conduct Annual Strategy Review:* At the start of the third year, the initial strategy has been achieved and the corporate strategy requires updating. The executive committee lists ten strategic issues. Each business unit is asked to develop a position on each issue as a prelude to updating its strategy and scorecard. *(months 25 - 26)*

13	14	15	16	17	18	19	20	21	22	23	24	25	26

6A *Communicate the Balanced Scorecard to the Entire Company:* At the end of one year, when the management teams are comfortable with the strategic approach, the scorecard is disseminated to the entire organization. *(month 12 - ongoing)*

6B *Establish Individual Performance Objectives:* The top three layers of management link their individual objectives and incentive compensation to their scorecards. *(months 13 - 14)*

8 *Conduct Monthly and Quarterly Reviews:* After corporate approval of the business unit scorecards, a monthly review process, supplemented by quarterly reviews that focus more heavily on strategic issues, begins. *(month 18 - ongoing)*

10 *Link Everyone's Performance to the Balanced Scorecard:* All employees are asked to link their individual objectives to the balanced scorecard. The entire organization's incentive compensation is linked to the scorecard. *(months 25 - 26)*

Note: Steps 7, 8, 9, and 10 are performed on a regular schedule. The balanced scorecard is now a routine part of the management process.

balanced scorecard forced the bank's senior managers to arrive at a consensus and then to translate their vision into terms that had meaning to the people who would realize the vision.

Communicating and Linking

"The top ten people in the business now understand the strategy better than ever before. It's too bad," a senior executive of a major oil company complained, "that we can't put this in a bottle so that everyone could share it." With the balanced scorecard, he can.

One company we have worked with deliberately involved three layers of management in the creation of its balanced scorecard. The senior executive group formulated the financial and customer objectives. It then mobilized the talent and information in the next two levels of managers by having them formulate the internal-business-process and learning-and-growth objectives that would drive the achievement of the financial and customer goals. For example, knowing the importance of satisfying customers' expectations of on-time

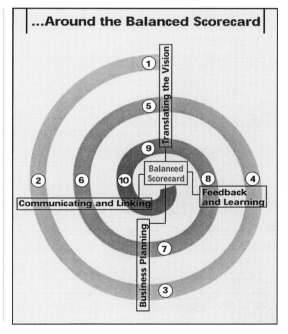

...Around the Balanced Scorecard

delivery, the broader group identified several internal business processes – such as order processing, scheduling, and fulfillment–in which the company had to excel. To do so, the company would have to retrain frontline employees and improve the information systems available to them. The group developed performance measures for those critical processes and for staff and systems capabilities.

Broad participation in creating a scorecard takes longer, but it offers several advantages: Information from a larger number of managers is incorporated into the internal objectives; the managers gain a better understanding of the company's long-term strategic goals; and such broad participation builds a stronger commitment to achieving those goals. But getting managers to buy into the scorecard is only a first step in linking individual actions to corporate goals.

The balanced scorecard signals to everyone what the organization is trying to achieve for shareholders and customers alike. But to align employees' individual performances with the overall strategy, scorecard users generally engage in three activities: communicating and educating, setting goals, and linking rewards to performance measures.

Communicating and Educating. Implementing a strategy begins with educating those who have to execute it. Whereas some organizations opt to hold their strategy close to the vest, most believe that they should disseminate it from top to bottom. A broad-based communication program shares with all employees the strategy and the critical objectives they have to meet if the strategy is to succeed.

The personal scorecard helps to communicate corporate and unit objectives to the people and teams performing the work.

Onetime events such as the distribution of brochures or newsletters and the holding of "town meetings" might kick off the program. Some organizations post bulletin boards that illustrate and explain the balanced scorecard measures, then update them with monthly results. Others use groupware and electronic bulletin boards to distribute the scorecard to the desktops of all employees and to encourage dialogue about the measures. The same media allow employees to make suggestions for achieving or exceeding the targets.

The balanced scorecard, as the embodiment of business unit strategy, should also be communicated upward in the organization–to corporate headquarters and to the corporate board of directors. With the scorecard, business units can quantify and communicate their long-term strategies to senior executives using a comprehensive set of linked financial and nonfinancial measures. Such communication informs the executives and the board in specific terms that long-term strategies designed for competitive success are in place. The measures also provide the basis for feedback and accountability. Meeting short-term financial targets should not constitute satisfactory performance when other measures indicate that the long-term strategy is either not working or not being implemented well.

Should the balanced scorecard be communicated beyond the boardroom to external shareholders? We believe that as senior executives gain confidence in the ability of the scorecard measures to monitor strategic performance and predict future financial performance, they will find ways to inform outside investors about those measures without disclosing competitively sensitive information.

Skandia, an insurance and financial services company based in Sweden, issues a supplement to its annual report called "The Business Navigator" – "an instrument to help us navigate into the future and thereby stimulate renewal and development." The supplement describes Skandia's strategy and the strategic measures the company uses to communicate and evaluate the strategy. It also provides a report on the company's performance along those measures during the year. The measures are customized for each operating unit and include, for example, market share, customer satisfaction and retention, employee competence, employee empowerment, and technology deployment.

Communicating the balanced scorecard promotes commitment and accountability to the business's long-term strategy. As one executive at Metro Bank declared, "The balanced scorecard is both motivating and obligating."

Setting Goals. Mere awareness of corporate goals, however, is not enough to change many people's behavior. Somehow, the organization's high-level strategic objectives and measures must be translated into objectives and measures for operating units and individuals.

The exploration group of a large oil company developed a technique to enable and encourage individuals to set goals for themselves that were consis-

80

The Personal Scorecard

Corporate Objectives

☐ Double our corporate value in seven years.
☐ Increase our earnings by an average of 20% per year.
☐ Achieve an internal rate of return 2% above the cost of capital.
☐ Increase both production and reserves by 20% in the next decade.

Corporate Targets					Scorecard Measures	Business Unit Targets					Team/Individual Objectives and Initiatives
1995	1996	1997	1998	1999		1995	1996	1997	1998	1999	1.
					Financial						
100	120	160	180	250	Earnings (in millions of dollars)						
100	450	200	210	225	Net cash flow						
100	85	80	75	70	Overhead and operating expenses						2.
					Operating						
100	75	73	70	64	Production costs per barrel						
100	97	93	90	82	Development costs per barrel						
100	105	108	108	110	Total annual production						3.

Team/Individual Measures	Targets	
1.		
2.		
3.		4.
4.		
5.		
Name:		5.
Location:		

tent with the organization's. It created a small, fold-up personal scorecard that people could carry in their shirt pockets or wallets. (See the exhibit "The Personal Scorecard.") The scorecard contains three levels of information. The first describes corporate objectives, measures, and targets. The second leaves room for translating corporate targets into targets for each business unit. For the third level, the company asks both individuals and teams to articulate which of their own objectives would be consistent with the business unit and corporate objectives, as well as what initiatives they would take to achieve their objectives. It also asks them to define up to five performance measures for their objectives and to set targets for each measure. The personal scorecard helps to communicate corporate and business unit objectives to the people and teams performing the work, enabling them to translate the objectives into meaningful tasks and targets for themselves. It also lets them keep that information close at hand – in their pockets.

Linking Rewards to Performance Measures. Should compensation systems be linked to balanced scorecard measures? Some companies, believing that tying financial compensation to performance is a powerful lever, have moved quickly to establish such a linkage. For example, an oil company that we'll call Pioneer Petroleum uses its scorecard as the sole basis for computing incentive compensation. The company ties 60% of its executives' bonuses to their achievement of ambitious targets for a weighted average of four financial indicators: return on capital, profitability, cash flow, and operating cost. It bases the remaining 40% on indicators of customer satisfaction, dealer satisfaction, employee satisfaction, and environmental responsibility (such as a percentage change in the level of emissions to water and air). Pioneer's CEO says that linking compensation to the scorecard has helped to align the company with its strategy. "I know of no competitor," he says, "who has this degree of alignment. It is producing results for us."

As attractive and as powerful as such linkage is, it nonetheless carries risks. For instance, does the company have the right measures on the scorecard? Does it have valid and reliable data for the selected measures? Could unintended or unexpected consequences arise from the way the targets for the measures are achieved? Those are questions that companies should ask.

Furthermore, companies traditionally handle multiple objectives in a compensation formula by assigning weights to each objective and calculating incentive compensation by the extent to which each weighted objective was achieved. This practice permits substantial incentive compensation to be paid if the business unit overachieves on a few objectives even if it falls far short on others. A better approach would be to establish minimum threshold levels for a critical subset of the strategic measures. Individuals would earn no incentive compensation if performance in a given period fell short of any threshold. This requirement should motivate people to achieve a more balanced performance across short- and long-term objectives.

Some organizations, however, have reduced their emphasis on short-term, formula-based incentive systems as a result of introducing the balanced scorecard. They have discovered that dialogue among executives and managers about the scorecard – both the formulation of the measures and objectives and the explanation of actual versus targeted results – provides a better opportunity to observe managers' performance and abilities. Increased knowledge of their managers' abilities makes it easier for executives to set incentive rewards subjectively and to defend those subjective evaluations – a process that is less susceptible to the game playing and distortions associated with explicit, formula-based rules.

One company we have studied takes an intermediate position. It bases bonuses for business unit managers on two equally weighted criteria: their achievement of a financial objective – economic value added – over a three-year period and a subjective assessment of their performance on measures drawn from the customer, internal-business-process, and learning-and-growth perspectives of the balanced scorecard.

That the balanced scorecard has a role to play in the determination of incentive compensation is not in doubt. Precisely what that role should be will become clearer as more companies experiment with linking rewards to scorecard measures.

Business Planning

"Where the rubber meets the sky": That's how one senior executive describes his company's long-range-planning process. He might have said the same of many other companies because their financially based management systems fail to link change programs and resource allocation to long-term strategic priorities.

The problem is that most organizations have separate procedures and organizational units for strategic planning and for resource allocation and budgeting. To formulate their strategic plans, senior executives go off-site annually and engage for several days in active discussions facilitated by senior planning and development managers or external consultants. The outcome of this exercise is a strategic plan articulating where the company expects (or hopes or prays) to be in three, five, and ten years. Typically, such plans then sit on executives' bookshelves for the next 12 months.

Meanwhile, a separate resource-allocation and budgeting process run by the finance staff sets financial targets for revenues, expenses, profits, and investments for the next fiscal year. The budget it produces consists almost entirely of financial numbers that generally bear little relation to the targets in the strategic plan.

Which document do corporate managers discuss in their monthly and quarterly meetings during the following year? Usually only the budget, because the periodic reviews focus on a comparison of actual and budgeted results for every line item. When is the strategic plan next discussed? Probably during the next annual off-site meeting, when the senior managers draw up a new set of three-, five-, and ten-year plans.

The very exercise of creating a balanced scorecard forces companies to integrate their strategic planning and budgeting processes and therefore helps to ensure that their budgets support their strategies. Scorecard users select measures of progress from all four scorecard perspectives and set targets for each of them. Then they determine which actions will drive them toward their targets, identify the measures they will apply to those drivers from the four perspectives, and establish the short-term milestones that will mark their progress along the strategic paths they have selected. Building a scorecard thus enables a company to link its financial budgets with its strategic goals.

For example, one division of the Style Company (not its real name) committed to achieving a seemingly impossible goal articulated by the CEO: to double revenues in five years. The forecasts built into the organization's existing strategic plan fell $1 billion short of this objective. The division's managers, after considering various scenarios, agreed to specific increases in five different performance drivers: the number of new stores opened, the number of new customers attracted into new and existing stores, the percentage of shoppers in each store converted into actual purchasers, the portion of existing customers retained, and average sales per customer.

By helping to define the key drivers of revenue growth and by committing to targets for each of them, the division's managers eventually grew comfortable with the CEO's ambitious goal.

The process of building a balanced scorecard – clarifying the strategic objectives and then identifying the few critical drivers – also creates a framework for managing an organization's various change programs. These initiatives – reengineering, employee empowerment, time-based management, and total quality management, among others – promise to deliver results but also compete with one another for scarce resources, including the scarcest resource of all: senior managers' time and attention.

Shortly after the merger that created it, Metro Bank, for example, launched more than 70 different initiatives. The initiatives were intended to produce a more competitive and successful institution, but they were inadequately integrated into the overall strategy. After building their balanced scorecard, Metro Bank's managers dropped many of those programs – such as a marketing effort directed at individuals with very high net worth – and consolidated others into initiatives that were better aligned with the company's strategic objectives. For example, the managers replaced a program aimed at enhancing existing low-level selling skills with a major initiative aimed at retraining salespersons to become trusted financial advisers, capable of selling a broad range of newly introduced products to the three selected customer segments. The bank made both changes because the scorecard enabled it to gain a better understanding of the programs required to achieve its strategic objectives.

Once the strategy is defined and the drivers are identified, the scorecard influences managers to concentrate on improving or reengineering those processes most critical to the organization's strategic success. That is how the scorecard most clearly links and aligns action with strategy.

The final step in linking strategy to actions is to establish specific short-term targets, or milestones,

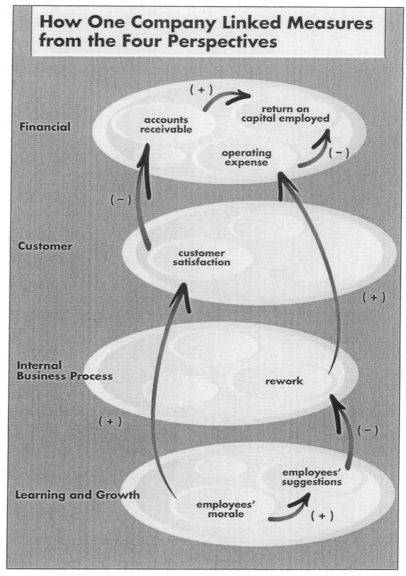

How One Company Linked Measures from the Four Perspectives

for the balanced scorecard measures. Milestones are tangible expressions of managers' beliefs about when and to what degree their current programs will affect those measures.

In establishing milestones, managers are expanding the traditional budgeting process to incorporate strategic as well as financial goals. Detailed financial planning remains important, but financial goals taken by themselves ignore the three other balanced scorecard perspectives. In an integrated planning and budgeting process, executives continue to budget for short-term financial performance, but they also introduce short-term targets for measures in the customer, internal-business-process, and learning-and-growth perspectives. With those milestones established, managers can continually test both the theory underlying the strategy and the strategy's implementation.

At the end of the business planning process, managers should have set targets for the long-term objectives they would like to achieve in all four scorecard perspectives; they should have identified the strategic initiatives required and allocated the necessary resources to those initiatives; and they should have established milestones for the measures that mark progress toward achieving their strategic goals.

Feedback and Learning

"With the balanced scorecard," a CEO of an engineering company told us, "I can continually test my strategy. It's like performing real-time research." That is exactly the capability that the scorecard should give senior managers: the ability to know at any point in its implementation whether the strategy they have formulated is, in fact, working, and if not, why.

The first three management processes – translating the vision, communicating and linking, and business planning – are vital for implementing strategy, but they are not sufficient in an unpredictable world. Together they form an important single-loop-learning process – single-loop in the sense that the objective remains constant, and any departure from the planned trajectory is seen as a defect to be remedied. This single-loop process does not require or even facilitate reexamination of either the strategy or the techniques used to implement it in light of current conditions.

Most companies today operate in a turbulent environment with complex strategies that, though valid when they were launched, may lose their validity as business conditions change. In this kind of environment, where new threats and opportunities arise constantly, companies must become capable of what Chris Argyris calls *double-loop learning* – learning that produces a change in people's assumptions and theories about cause-and-effect relationships. (See "Teaching Smart People How to Learn," HBR May-June 1991.)

Budget reviews and other financially based management tools cannot engage senior executives in double-loop learning – first, because these tools address performance from only one perspective, and second, because they don't involve strategic learning. Strategic learning consists of gathering feedback, testing the hypotheses on which strategy was based, and making the necessary adjustments.

The balanced scorecard supplies three elements that are essential to strategic learning. First, it articulates the company's shared vision, defining in clear and operational terms the results that the company, as a team, is trying to achieve. The scorecard communicates a holistic model that links individual efforts and accomplishments to business unit objectives.

Second, the scorecard supplies the essential strategic feedback system. A business strategy can be viewed as a set of hypotheses about cause-and-effect relationships. A strategic feedback system should be able to test, validate, and modify the hypotheses embedded in a business unit's strategy. By establishing short-term goals, or milestones, within the business planning process, executives are forecasting the relationship between changes in performance drivers and the associated changes in one or more specified goals. For example, executives at Metro Bank estimated the amount of time it would take for improvements in training and in the availability of information systems before employees could sell multiple financial products effectively to existing and new customers. They also estimated how great the effect of that selling capability would be.

Another organization attempted to validate its hypothesized cause-and-effect relationships in the balanced scorecard by measuring the strength of the linkages among measures in the different perspectives. (See the chart "How One Company Linked Measures from the Four Perspectives.") The company found significant correlations between employees' morale, a measure in the learning-and-growth perspective, and customer satisfaction, an important customer perspective measure. Customer satisfaction, in turn, was correlated with faster payment of invoices – a relationship that led to a substantial reduction in accounts receivable and hence a higher return on capital employed. The company also found correlations between employees' morale and the number of suggestions made by employees (two learning-and-growth measures) as well as between an increased number of suggestions and lower rework (an internal-business-process measure). Evidence of such strong correlations help to confirm the organization's business strategy. If, however, the expected correlations are not found over time, it should be an indication to executives that the theory underlying the unit's strategy may not be working as they had anticipated.

Especially in large organizations, accumulating sufficient data to document significant correlations and causation among balanced scorecard measures can take a long time – months or years. Over the short term, managers' assessment of strategic impact may have to rest on subjective and qualitative judgments. Eventually, however, as more evidence accumulates, organizations may be able to provide more objectively grounded estimates of cause-and-effect relationships. But just getting managers to think systematically about the assumptions underlying their strategy is an improvement over the current practice of making decisions based on short-term operational results.

Third, the scorecard facilitates the strategy review that is essential to strategic learning. Traditionally, companies use the monthly or quarterly meetings between corporate and division executives to analyze the most recent period's financial results. Discussions focus on past performance and on explanations of why financial objectives were not achieved. The balanced scorecard, with its specification of the causal relationships between performance drivers and objectives, allows corporate and business unit executives to use their periodic review sessions to evaluate the validity of the unit's strategy and the quality of its execution. If the unit's employees and managers have delivered on the performance drivers (retraining of employees, availability of information systems, and new financial products and services, for instance), then their failure to achieve the expected outcomes (higher sales to targeted customers, for example) signals that the theory underlying the strategy may not be valid. The disappointing sales figures are an early warning.

Managers should take such disconfirming evidence seriously and reconsider their shared conclusions about market conditions, customer value propositions, competitors' behavior, and internal capabilities. The result of such a review may be a decision to reaffirm their belief in the current strategy but to adjust the quantitative relationship among the strategic measures on the balanced scorecard. But they also might conclude that the unit needs a different strategy (an example of double-loop learning) in light of new knowledge about market conditions and internal capabilities. In any case, the scorecard will have stimulated key executives to learn about the viability of their strategy. This capacity for enabling organizational learning at the executive level – strategic learning – is what distinguishes the balanced scorecard, making it invaluable for those who wish to create a strategic management system.

Toward a New Strategic Management System

Many companies adopted early balanced-scorecard concepts to improve their performance measurement systems. They achieved tangible but narrow results. Adopting those concepts provided clarification, consensus, and focus on the desired improvements in performance. More recently, we have seen companies expand their use of the balanced scorecard, employing it as the foundation of an integrated and iterative strategic management system. Companies are using the scorecard to

☐ clarify and update strategy,
☐ communicate strategy throughout the company,
☐ align unit and individual goals with the strategy,
☐ link strategic objectives to long-term targets and annual budgets,
☐ identify and align strategic initiatives, and
☐ conduct periodic performance reviews to learn about and improve strategy.

The balanced scorecard enables a company to align its management processes and focuses the entire organization on implementing long-term strategy. At National Insurance, the scorecard provided the CEO and his managers with a central framework around which they could redesign each piece of the company's management system. And because of the cause-and-effect linkages inherent in the scorecard framework, changes in one component of the system reinforced earlier changes made elsewhere. Therefore, every change made over the 30-month period added to the momentum that kept the organization moving forward in the agreed-upon direction.

Without a balanced scorecard, most organizations are unable to achieve a similar consistency of vision and action as they attempt to change direction and introduce new strategies and processes. The balanced scorecard provides a framework for managing the implementation of strategy while also allowing the strategy itself to evolve in response to changes in the company's competitive, market, and technological environments. ▽

Reprint 96107   To place an order, call 1-800-545-7685.

2.4 Benchmarking: does your performance measure up?

Tony Brabazon and David Brabazon

Benchmarking works best when it is part of a well-defined strategy. An increasingly popular management tool, Tony Brabazon and David Brabazon explain where the concept came from and just what it involves.

What is benchmarking?

The term 'benchmark' originally referred to a surveyor's mark used as a reference point in either topographical surveys or tidal measurements. In recent times, the term benchmarking has gained wide currency in the business world as being the "process of comparing a firm's products, services or business practices against those of its toughest competitors or those of companies recognised as industry leaders". By benchmarking such metrics as percentage of orders delivered on-time, warranty claim rate, repeat purchase rate and administration cost per order (to name but a few) against those of its competitors, a firm can determine where it can improve its products or operations in order to enhance its competitive position.

Surveys suggest that the formal use of benchmarking in both the US and the UK is widespread. A 1995 survey[1] conducted in the US suggested that more than 70% of Fortune 500 companies used benchmarking on a regular basis. A 1996 UK survey[2] performed by the DTI and the CBI produced similar results. Out of 600 companies surveyed, 62% claimed to practice benchmarking.

Old wine in new bottles?

Benchmarking is not a new idea. Accountants have long assessed the financial health of companies using ratio analysis, in effect benchmarking a company's current period ratios against either historical ratios or ratios of peer companies. In a wider setting, people and companies have always observed and copied good ideas and practices developed by others. The development of Just-In-Time (JIT) production provides a good example of such imitation. The idea was sparked by a trip to the US by Taiichi Ohno of Toyota shortly after the Second World War. He observed the way US supermarkets stocked their shelves overnight to meet the following day's demand and translated the idea into a JIT approach to manufacturing.

Although the basic concept underlying benchmarking is by no means revolutionary, it was (and is!) often implemented in an informal manner. Good ideas would be copied on a haphazard basis but with no formal process to actively seek out innovative ideas which could be implemented by the firm to increase both efficiency and effectiveness. A more formal approach to benchmarking seeks to ensure that managers continually assess their firm's performance using both external and internal metrics and it encourages firms to continually question the current design of their production or service processes.

Types of benchmarking studies

Many different benchmark studies can be performed. Any activity whose output can be measured can be benchmarked. A benchmark study could focus on:

- business processes (either production or support)
- products (performance, quality, customer perception, rate of innovation)
- customers (market share by segment, customer retention rates)
- staff (age, qualification, experience)

A study could be performed in-house, for example where a firm has several divisions, between firms in the same industry or between firms in different industries which share similar processes or problems. As an example of an in-house study, the European division of Xerox implemented a benchmarking project to boost sales revenues. By comparing the performance of sales forces in each country, valuable information such as which countries sold the largest proportion of high margin colour copiers and which countries had the lowest customer attrition rates was uncovered. This information was then used to improve the performance of the lower performing sales regions.

The comparison of processes between firms in differing industries can reveal opportunities to obtain, at least a temporary, competitive advantage. In the airline business, aircraft utilisation and load factors are major determinants of profitability. One of the key drivers of aircraft utilisation is the turnaround time between flights. When the low-cost US airline, Southwest, wanted to assess the performance of its refuelling processes it found that it was already amongst the best in the airline business. Rather than resting on its laurels, it benchmarked itself against the refuelling performance of Formula One pit crews. The lessons learnt from the benchmarking study led to a re-design of the refuelling procedures which resulted in a drop in average refuelling time from 40 to 12 minutes.[2]

The five steps of benchmarking

Benchmarking projects can range in scale from the benchmarking of a single process to the benchmarking of the entire manufacturing or service activities of a firm. Regardless of the scale of the project, it will generally proceed through five discrete stages:

1 Internal study and preliminary competitive analysis

2   Fostering of a commitment to the benchmarking project and building the benchmark team

3   Identification of benchmark partners

4   Information gathering and sharing

5   Initiation of action to achieve or exceed the competitive benchmark.

The first step in benchmarking is to decide which activities of the organization are to be investigated. Initial studies should focus on the critical success factors of the organization. What areas represent the greatest portion of the firm's total costs or value-added? Alternatively, what issues are critical in the eyes of the firm's customers? To help identify which areas may be suitable for an in-depth benchmarking project, a preliminary study may be performed by collecting internal data on the firm's processes and comparing this against readily available external data.

A large scale benchmarking project can take months or perhaps even years from the instigation of the initial study to the final implementation of the identified process improvements. This requires a long-term commitment by both senior management and the members of the benchmarking team. Successful project management requires that clear objectives and deadlines be set for the benchmarking team. The team should be multidisciplinary to ensure that there is commitment to the project across several departments.

Once the benchmark team has been assembled, the next step is to select benchmark partners. If the firm is currently uncompetitive, initial benchmarking studies usually tend to concentrate on direct competitors of the firms in an effort to close the gap with these firms. As the competitiveness of the firm improves, benchmarking efforts will tend to shift towards gaining competitive advantage and will naturally expand in focus to include high-performing companies in other sectors.

When benchmark partners have been selected, collection of the required benchmark information begins. The information may be collected unilaterally from a variety of sources such as trade association journals, press releases, interviews with customers and suppliers, conference papers, patent filings or the published accounts of the chosen firms. Alternatively, benchmark information may be obtained on a co-operative basis through direct contact with the other firm(s). Whilst direct contact between firms is likely to result in better quality benchmarking information, firms, particularly direct competitors, are likely to be wary of disclosing sensitive operating data to each other. In these cases, benchmarking may still be possible through an independent third party. If several firms agree to participate in a benchmark study, an independent party can collect and audit detailed data from each benchmarking participant and then share a summarised, anonymous version of this information with all of the participants.

There are several specialist benchmarking intermediary firms that have extensive experience in planning and conducting benchmark studies. The best known examples include the International

Benchmarking Clearing House (based in Houston, USA), the Benchmarking Competency Centre (based in Milwaukee, USA) and the Strategic Planning Institute Council on Benchmarking (based in Cambridge, Massachusetts, USA). In the UK, the Chartered Institute of Management Accountants maintains a Benchmarking Contacts Register that contains in excess of 150 potential benchmarking contacts.

The collection of benchmark data should represent the 'real' start rather than the end of the benchmarking process. Once the data is obtained, the firm can assess the severity of any performance gaps identified in respect of the items being benchmarked.

The findings of the benchmark study should be communicated to all staff involved. Although this can be a painful process if performance is found to be poor, the study will provide objective data on outside methods of operation. This may ultimately reduce the resistance to change as employees are given clear insight as to where their firm's performance is weak.

If the benchmarking process is to be of longer-term benefit, imitating competitor processes or ideas is not sufficient. Ultimately, the process must stimulate a review of the firm's processes and lead to creative thinking as to how these individual processes (and the linkages between the processes) could be improved. After the plans for improvement have been drawn up and implemented, the benchmark process should be repeated to determine whether the firm has managed to achieve its new targets for the benchmarked processes. Some firms view the implementation of a benchmarking process as an on-going, rather than as a one off productivity project. The project is considered to be a tool to focus attention on continuous improvement of operations, in other words, 'as a journey rather than a destination'.

Linkages between benchmarking and other cost management techniques

Although benchmarking studies can be applied to the revenue generation activities of firms, they are often most closely identified with productivity improvement and cost reduction. There are three distinct stages of cost management activities in the life of a typical product or service. Cost management in the initial product/service design process, cost management during the production cycle and cost management during the post-sale and disposal cycle. Activities in each of these stages can be the subject of separate benchmarking studies.

Benchmarking can be linked to activity-based management. Activity-based costing provides raw information on the cost of each of the firm's activities (processes). This information can serve as a reference point in assessing the financial benefits of improving performance on operational benchmarks.

Linkages can also be drawn between benchmarking and total quality management (TQM). TQM focuses on the continuous improvement of a firm's products and processes. TQM efforts can be assisted by information uncovered by benchmarking, as this will help highlight where the firms should focus its improvement efforts.

Limitations of benchmarking

Although benchmark studies can provide useful information for both planning and performance evaluation, practical difficulties can emerge in the benchmarking process. There is no guarantee that it will be easy to get high quality, comparable benchmark information. Benchmarking contains an implicit suggestion that the strategies of the firm and that of its benchmark partners are similar. If the firms are pursuing widely varying strategies, the critical success factors and the relative importance of individual business processes within each firm will differ. Consequently, the comparability of benchmark data will be reduced.

A benchmarking study is only meaningful in the context of a well – defined strategy or else it just results in 'follow the leader' behaviour. Merely copying good business practices of successful firms may temporarily improve a firm's cost position but it will not generate any enduring advantage. The efficiency of business processes is a necessary but not sufficient condition for long term success. Benchmarking in itself will not help develop new, attractive product or service offerings.

Some commentators have voiced concerns regarding the basic philosophy which underlies benchmarking. There is a danger that benchmarking the performance of individual products or business processes may lead to incrementalist thinking. The best way to improve a process may be to reconsider the design of the entire process (the principle underlying business process re-engineering) rather than attempting to optimise each component of that process through benchmarking. However, it could also be argued that the benchmarking process, by focusing attention on the efficiency or otherwise of the firm's operations could provide the creative stimulus for redesign of business processes. Ultimately the balance of the argument depends on the quality of the firm's managers. Are managers likely to blindly attempt to improve benchmark performance without considering possibilities for broader process re-design?

Finally, the idea of benchmarking is best suited to stable environments. If a firm is operating in a business environment which is characterised by rapid change of products and business processes, the value of historical benchmark information is likely to be low.

Despite these limitations, benchmarking, whether performed formally or informally, can be a useful tool for maintaining and enhancing the efficiency and effectiveness of an organization. Benchmarking provides an objective, external assessment of the current performance of an organization's activities and should help stimulate a more creative outlook on 'how best to do things'.

1 Elmuti D., Kathawala Y. and Lloyd S. (1997) The benchmarking process: assessing its value and limitations, *Industrial management*, July–August vol 39(4): 12–19.

2 Murdoch A. (1997) Lateral benchmarking, *Management Today*, November pg 64–68.

Source: *Accountancy Ireland*, October 2000, Vol. 32, No. 5, pp. 16–17

2.5 Is there a 'correct' method of investment appraisal?

David Dugdale

David Dugdale of Bristol Business School studies the different methods of investment appraisal and suggests that the management accountant should have a thorough understanding of all of them if they are to be wisely used.

Investment appraisal is a key element of management accounting and a thorough understanding of the techniques of investment appraisal is very important. Textbooks compare the techniques of accounting rate of return, payback, net present value and internal rate of return, recommending net present value as the soundest technique. Here the arguments will be reviewed and it will be concluded that the choice of technique in practice should not be as clear cut as is sometimes suggested.

Accounting rate of return

Accounting rate of return is calculated in basically the same way as 'return on investment' as:

$$\frac{\text{Profit}}{\text{Investment}}$$

but whether 'profit' is before or after interest charges and whether 'investment' is the initial outlay or is averaged over the life of the project is unclear.

This lack of clarity seems strange. The point of this technique is that it is based on the same principles as the published financial statements. Companies (and managers) are often evaluated by the 'return on investment' or 'return on capital employed' ratio derived from published Profit and Loss Account and Balance Sheet. (The two ratios are identical, merely reflecting the two sides of the Balance Sheet: 'capital employed' reflects the financing of business, 'investment' reflects the use of that finance). It is therefore logical that it should be calculated in a way which makes it comparable with theses ratios. As the Balance Sheet contains written down asset values one would expect accounting rate of return to be calculated as:

$$\frac{\text{Profit}}{\text{Average (written down) investment}}$$

And this accords with common sense because if profit is after depreciation then one would expect that depreciation to affect the value of the investment. Following the same principle (that the numerator and denominator must be comparable) allows other difficulties to be resolved. If we are measuring management's performance the ratio would be:

$$\frac{\text{Profit before interest and tax}}{\text{Average (total) capital employed}}$$

but if we were measuring return to shareholders the ratio would be:

$$\frac{\text{Profit after interest and tax}}{\text{Shareholders' funds}}$$

We must compare 'return' with the funds (or investment) which generate that return.

The following simple example will be used to compare accounting rate of return with other techniques:

			£000
Investment			(100)
Cash flow	Year	1	20
		2	30
		3	40
		4	40
		5	10

Straight-line depreciation of £20,000 per year over the five-year life of the asset would mean reported profits of:

		£000
Year	1	–
	2	10
	3	20
	4	20
	5	(10)

Average profit would be £8,000 per year. Average investment would be £50,000 (as the investment declines in value over the five years due to the depreciation charge) and accounting rate of return would be:

$$\frac{8,000}{50,000} = 16\%$$

Payback

Payback is a simple investment-appraisal technique which involves determining how long will be needed before the initial investment is 'paid back'. Unlike accounting rate of return which is bound by accounting definitions of 'profit' and 'investment', payback concentrates on the specific *cash flows* which an investment will generate. (In this respect payback is superior to accounting rate of return because the management accounting theory of decision making is based on the simple concept that financial advice should be based on whether the wealth of the decision-maker will be increased if a particular decision is taken. The definitions and conventions of financial accounting should not be allowed to muddy the waters of this essentially simple problem.)

The well documented drawbacks of the payback technique are based on the fact that future cash flows, in themselves, do not indicate increased wealth. This is because a money flow in the future is not worth as much as the same money flow now. (Cash available now can be invested and so is worth more than the same cash flow at a later date.)

The disadvantages of payback:

- all cash flows within the payback period are given equal weight
- cash flows outside the payback period are ignored.

Although one might expect payback to be little used because of these disadvantages, in practice, it is used extensively! Its simplicity probably explains its popularity:

- decision-makers understand information presented to them
- calculations are straightforward and likely to be error-free
- since data is itself unreliable (estimates of future cash flows) sophisticated analysis may not be justified.

Payback can also be recommended if the business requires liquid funds at some date in the future – a project which 'pays back' before this date would be preferable to one which needs to be funded for a longer period. A further advantage is the 'risk aversion' of payback and this will be discussed later.

Payback period in our example would be 3.25 years. If the stipulated payback period were longer than this the investment would be accepted, if not, it would be rejected.

Discounting techniques – net present value

The recommended approach is to calculate the 'net present value' of a proposed investment by 'discounting' future cash flows to present value and summing (or 'netting') them together. The present value of a future cash flow is calculated by multiplying it by the factor

$$\frac{1}{(1+r)^n}$$

where r is the discount rate and n is the number of periods (usually years) in the future when the cash flow will take place.

'Discounting' is the opposite of 'compounding' and, remembering that a principal, P, will grow to an amount, A, after n years if invested at a rate of interest r, we have

$$A = P(1+r)^n$$

and

$$P = \frac{A}{(1+r)^n}$$

We can say that P grows to A in n years or, equivalently, that the future cash flow A is worth P in *present value* terms. By discounting future cash flows the problem of the time value of money is eliminated and, if the net present value is positive (inflows in present-value terms exceed outflows in present-value terms) the project can be recommended.

In practice NPV calculations are easy because tables of discount factors are readily available. In our example, assuming a discount rate of 10 per cent per annum:

Year	Cash flow £000	Factor	Present value £000
0	(100)	1.000	(100.0)
1	20	0.909	18.2
2	30	0.826	24.8
3	40	0.751	30.0
4	40	0.683	27.3
5	10	0.621	6.2
			6.5

If the *cost of capital* were 10 per cent this project could be recommended because it generates a positive NPV of £6,500. One interpretation of NPV is that, if the project were financed by a loan at 10 per cent per annum, the interest on the loan and the original capital could be repaid out of project cash flows and this would eventually leave a cash balance at the end of the project worth £6,500 *in present value terms*.

The net present value technique is the academic recommendation and it is theoretically sound. However, its use in practice implies that the decision-maker must judge a project by an *absolute* number and while it is easy to give the 'rule' – any project generating positive NPV is acceptable – a decision maker will be interested not only in the final NPV 'payoff' but also in the size of the initial investment and the length of time before the project 'matures'.

Use the NPV rule becomes problematic if capital is 'rationed', because not all projects can then be accepted. In this situation it becomes necessary to rank projects according to their 'earning power' – placing the project which generates the maximum NPV per pound invested at the top of the list. Conventionally the *profitability index* is calculated in order to rank projects, where:

$$\text{Profitability index} = \frac{\text{NPV of cash inflows}}{\text{Investment outflow}}$$

In our example:

$$\text{Profitability index} = \frac{106.5}{100} = 1.065$$

This project would rank behind a project with profitability index of 1.1 but ahead of a project with profitability index of 1.05.

A common source of confusion and misunderstanding in NPV calculations is the treatment of inflation. Typically, the discount rate is the *money* cost of capital, i.e. the rate payable on borrowed money (the source of the funds may be a bank, debentures, equity or some combination of sources). Such a rate *includes* an allowance for

* Strictly the 'money' cost of capital is given by $(1 + r)(1 + I) - 1$ where r is the 'real' cost of capital and I the rate of inflation. If inflation is assumed to be 8% then a 'money' cost of capital of 5% implies a real return of 6.5%.

inflation in the sense that the lender cannot expect any more than the interest rate. (The lender may charge a 15 per cent rate assuming that inflation will be 8 per cent and so a 7 per cent 'real return' will be generated).*

If a money cost of capital is employed then the cash flows on which the analysis is performed should also *include* any inflation which is expected. (And, if different rates of inflation are expected on revenues and costs then this should be reflected in the cash flows.)

In practice, cash flows are often projected in so called 'real' terms, i.e. excluding inflation. Given the uncertain nature of estimated future cash flows this is not surprising, inflating 'guesstimated' future cash flows may give even the most determined accountant pause for thought! And, since inflation might be expected to affect all companies equally, it can reasonably be assumed that, if there are unexpected inflationary pressures, they will be compensated by price adjustments.

There are therefore compelling reasons for the use of cash flows in 'real' terms in NPV analysis. However, it therefore follows that the discount rate should also be in 'real' terms.

Any inflation element in the cost of capital should be *excluded* from the discount rate before proceeding with the analysis. It would not be surprising if this important point were overlooked in practice and a survey by Carsberg and Hope (1976) showed that this was indeed the case.

Discounting techniques – internal rate of return

An alternative approach, still based on discounting principles, is the calculation of 'internal rate of return' – that discount rate at which the net present value of the project is zero. The decision rule now becomes – accept the project if its internal rate of return (IRR) is greater than the cost of capital, reject if the IRR is less than the cost of capital. If a decision has to be made about a single project with 'conventional' cash flows (i.e. a single outlay followed by a series of inflows) IRR will lead to the same decision as NPV. However, in more complex circumstances IRR and NPV can lead to different decisions and IRR generally receives a bad press for a number of reasons. These are:

Calculation is complex

In our example the IRR might be calculated as follows – by trying a different discount rate – say 15 per cent:

Year	Cash flow £000	Factor	Present value £000
0	(100)	1.000	(100.0)
1	20	0.870	17.4
2	30	0.756	22.7
3	40	0.658	26.3
4	40	0.572	22.9
5	10	0.497	5.0
			(5.7)

And a linear approximation allows the discount rate where NPV is zero to be calculated:

$$\text{IRR} = 10\% + \frac{6.5}{12.2} \times 5\% = 12.7\%$$

The calculation appears both messy and approximate. Nevertheless neither of these criticisms are fair. The existence of powerful spreadsheets such as Lotus 1-2-3 and Excel allows IRR to be calculated instantly and accurately by using the relevant function.

There may be multiple IRRs

If project cash flows reverse during the life of the project – there may, for example, be an initial outflow followed by several inflows before another major outflow (as plant undergoes major refurbishment, for example) – there may be more than one IRR. A graph of discount versus NPV might appear as follows:

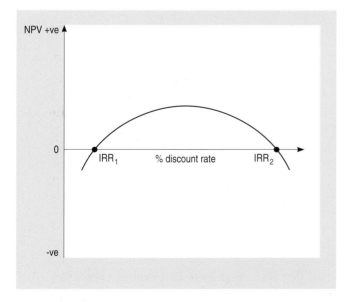

In such an example the IRR decision rule (accept if cost of capital is less than IRR) is misleading because the project should only be accepted if cost of capital is *between* IRR_1 and IRR_2.

To explain this result it is necessary to understand the *re-investment assumptions* implicit in the NPV and IRR calculations. All NPV calculations assume that incoming cash can be re-invested at the rate which is used in the NPV calculations. This means that the calculation of IRR_1 assumes reinvestment at IRR_1 while the calculation of IRR_2 assumes re-investment at IRR_2. Only at rates between IRR_1 and IRR_2 can the incoming cash be re-invested at a rate which is sufficient to offset both the initial cash outflow and the eventual second cash outflow. This analysis is perfectly sound and, arguably, the project is only acceptable if the cost of capital lies between IRR_1 and IRR_2. Unfortunately, however, it means that the IRR decision rule – accept if cost of capital is less than IRR – can only be applied to projects having conventional cash flows.

The NPV approach avoids this problem quite simply. By using the cost of capital as the discount rate in the NPV formula a negative NPV is generated if cost of capital is less than IRR_1, a positive NPV is obtained if cost of capital is between IRR_1 and IRR_2, and the NPV is negative again if cost of capital is greater that IRR_2.

The possibility of multiple IRRs is cited as a disadvantage of the IRR technique. However, the problem can be overcome. Multiple IRRs arise only when cash flows reverse more than once. In these circumstances it is only necessary to identify the (possibly) several IRRs (some calculators will draw the graph of NPV versus discount rate in a few seconds) and draw the correct conclusions.

IRR is inappropriate if projects are mutually exclusive

The third problem concerns the selection of a favoured project from two or more projects which 'mutually exclusive' (i.e. if one is chosen the others are automatically ruled out). Suppose that, instead of our project (A) being a simple accept/reject decision we have to choose between it and another project (B) which can be compared with project A as follows:

	Project A	Project B
Initial investment (£000)	100	50
Net present value (£000)	6.5	5.0
Internal rate of return (%)	12.7	18.0

The internal rate of return approach would favour project B (18.0 per cent compared with 12.7 per cent), however, provided funds are freely available project A would maximize wealth because, if chosen, it could generate £6,500 NPV compared with project B's £5,000. In essence, IRR can mislead because it may select a lower investment with higher 'earning potential', when it may be preferable to invest a greater sum which generates a lower 'return' but (because of its scale) produces a greater sum in the end.

The last objection does mean that IRR must be used with caution, if a choice has to be made between mutually exclusive projects. And NPV is usually recommended in preference to IRR because of the three objections discussed above and a much more subtle point concerning the reinvestment assumptions implicit in the two methods.

Whilst the IRR technique assumes that cash flows can be re-invested at the IRR, the NPV technique assumes that cash flows can be re-invested at the cost of capital used in the discounting process. This difference has two repercussions:

1   Even if mutually exclusive projects have the *same initial investment* (so the third objection raised against the IRR does not apply) NPV and IRR can give conflicting results. IRR may prefer a project with high early cash flows (assumed re-invested at the IRR) whilst NPV may prefer a different project – with higher flows later.

2   If IRR is used to rank projects in a capital-rationing situation the ranking may be different from that obtained by using profitability index because IRR will favour early cash inflows (assuming re-investment at the IRR) whilst profitability index (being based on NPV) may produce a different ranking.

It is usually assumed that NPV (and its derivative, the profitability index) provide the best guidance because the cost of capital re-investment assumption is more conservative and likely to be more realistic.

Discussion of techniques

First, it is by no means certain that the NPV method is definitely better than the IRR approach. It is certainly conceivable that the IRR re-investment assumption is as realistic as the NPV assumption – any business which could only invest its funds at the cost of capital would not be in business for long! And, in a capital-rationing situation there may be other projects readily available which would generate returns well in excess of the cost of capital. The IRR re-investment assumption could be more realistic in this situation and a technique which favours early inflows (as IRR does) could be preferable because it makes finance available with which to fund other projects. The point can also be made that the technique which favours early inflows is also more risk averse – because earlier cash flows are more certain than later ones.

Having defended IRR on theoretical grounds it can be pointed out that it is, arguably more 'meaningful' than NPV. A manager presented with an NPV of £6,500 may well ask what this figure 'means' – what investment? How long? etc. – an absolute number cannot easily be assessed in isolation. The same manager presented with an IRR of 12.7 per cent immediately has a 'feel' for the project – if money can be borrowed at, say, 5 per cent, then the project is probably sound. If the cost of the capital is 10 per cent then there does not appear to be much margin for error.

These considerations are borne out in practice. A survey by Pike (1980), reported by Pike and Dobbins (1986), revealed that 41 per cent of firms surveyed used IRR as their primary method of investment appraisal compared with only 17 per cent which used NPV as their primary method.

To sum up, IRR is criticized because it is complex, there may be multiple IRRs, it can mislead where projects are mutually exclusive and its re-investment assumption may be optimistic. Nevertheless, provided that the method is thoroughly understood, none of these objections is insuperable and there are reasons why IRR may be preferred to NPV.

It is interesting to compare the result obtained using IRR with that produced by the accounting rate of return (ARR) method. Remember that the accounting rate of return was 16 per cent but the IRR was 12.7 per cent. This is typical. On the basis of ARR it may appear that the project is profitable if the cost of capital is, say, 14 per cent. However, this is erroneous; the project is only viable if the cost of capital is less than 12.7 per cent.

Note that the IRR and the ARR are comparable but IRR is less than ARR. This is what one would expect because ARR treats all future inflows as equally valuable whilst IRR takes account of the time value of money. If ARR were calculated in other ways, for example based on initial investment rather than average (depreciated) investment, the comparison between IRR and ARR would not make sense.

Given that accounting rate of return does not take account of the time value of money, one might assume that it should not be used. However, this does not necessarily follow. Remembering that analysts often use return on investment to evaluate business performance, a change on the ROI ratio could actually affect the company's share price!

If an investment were big enough to have repercussions on published P & L and Balance Sheet it would be foolish not to calculate the ARR!

Having made a case for at least considering IRR and ARR we can consider the payback technique. As discussed earlier, payback is often used in practice, probably because of its simplicity.

However, it may also be used because of its risk aversion – early cash flows are given full value, late cash flows are ignored.

The usual textbook advice is to take account of risk in both the following ways:

1   If payback is used by decreasing the required payback period.

2   If the IRR is used by increasing the required 'hurdle rate'.

3   If NPV is used by increasing the discount rate to take account of the 'risk' associated with the project. The capital asset pricing model provides a means of assessing the premium which ought to be added to the 'risk free' discount rate.

4   To assign probabilities to 'best', 'more likely' and 'worst' values for each variable and calculate a range of possible outcomes together with their probabilities. (This approach can be refined by establishing distributions for the input variables and 'simulating' the project many times in order to build up a distribution of possible outcomes).

The relatively straightforward methods of handling risk if payback or IRR are used are cited as advantages of these techniques. However, none of the techniques described above deals with the important point that early cash flows are likely to be more certain than late ones. The discounting techniques take account of the time value of money but they assume that whatever cash flows are projected are *certain*. Only the payback technique clearly favours early cash flows much more than late ones and this may partially account for its popularity. (The IRR approach favours early inflows when compared with the NPV approach because of its re-investment assumption. However, this is a very fine point compared with payback which ignores late cash flows altogether.)

Conclusion

It could be argued that much of the discussion is so academic as to be irrelevant in practice. Studies of investment decision-making in practice reveal that financial analysis is only part of the decision-making process and social factors are equally important. However, accepting this point and the need for a rounded, pragmatic, approach to investment decisions does not excuse management accountants from thoroughly understanding the tools of their trade.

The arguments put forward here suggest that *all* the techniques of investment appraisal need to be well understood if they are to be wisely used. In summary:

1   NPV is the principal theoretical recommendation and should be used if the cost of capital is a realistic re-investment assumption.

2   IRR, like NPV, incorporates discounting principles and, for some managers, may be more obviously meaningful than the absolute NPV of the project. However, IRR needs to be thoroughly understood because of possible difficulties concerning multiple IRRs and its use if projects are mutually exclusive.

3   Payback if much used in practice and, aside from its obvious simplicity, it can also be recommended if a risk-averse decision is needed (or if liquidity is a major problem).

4   ARR takes no account of the time value of money and could lead to an incorrect decision if compared with the cost of capital. However, because of the extensive use of the return on capital employed or return on investment ratio in practice it could be foolish not to calculate it.

The analysis suggests that there may be a place for all the techniques of investment appraisal in the management accountant's armoury. However, a thorough understanding of their theoretical nuances is important.

References

Carsberg, B. V. and Hope, A. (1976) *Business Investment Decisions under Inflation*, Institute of Chartered Accountants in England and Wales.

Pike, R. H. and Dobbins, R. (1986) *Investment Decisions and Financial Strategy*, Philip Allan, p. 274.

Source: *Management Accounting*, May 1991

3.1 Anita Roddick: adventurer

Interviewed by Ronnie Lessem

All our early recipes were natural and earthy including seaweed, nettles, orchids, henna ... Our shops are like a cross between a chemistry set and a toyshop. You can try anything ...

Anita Roddick, Director, Body Shop

I've always worked terribly hard. From the age of ten, when my father died, there was no alternative but to work for survival and that never leaves one. My parents were Italian immigrants to this country. My father had been interned, during the war, and we children were sent to a Catholic school. Being foreign set us apart.

My mother ran a restaurant café in a coastal resort in Sussex. The cafés in the fifties played the part of modern youth clubs. In fact, before he died, my father had installed the first juke box in a café in this area. I used to change the décor about to make the atmosphere in the café more pleasant. I loved playing about with the display, especially in the soda fountain bar. It was great theatre. In retrospect, this background must have done me an enormous amount of good.

After school I went on to college. I was training to be a teacher. The same showground. During the holidays I used to work at Butlins, from six in the morning to twelve at night, to earn more money. I seem to have inexhaustible energy.

At college I had this extraordinary lecturer in aesthetics. He showed us ways of presentation, of understatement and overstatement. I went on to teach history, and was lucky to have this amazingly free-thinking headmaster. He let me do anything. I created my own special classroom atmosphere evoking the subject we were covering with the music and visual art forms of the period. The kids became totally involved.

So I did well as a teacher – it's all theatre, you know, all acting – but I wanted to go to Geneva, and work for the United Nations. I had such gall in those days that I just appeared on their doorstep and got a job in the women's section of the International Labour Organization. Having made lots of money, tax free, I decided to travel around the world, to North Africa, India, Australia, South America and Polynesia. What preoccupied me was the local women's skin. In those hot places it should have been dry and crèpy, but it was like satin. In Tahiti, for instance, it didn't take me long to work out why. Women rubbed their bodies with a lump of stuff that looked like lard. It was cocoa butter. In Morocco women were washing their gorgeous silky hair in mud. In Mexico, I saw a mother treat her child's burn by snapping off a cactus leaf and applying the slimy juice – aloes – to his skin. When I returned to England I started looking around for these natural products. I had no luck, and my interest waned.

In the meantime, in exotic Littlehampton, I had met my husband to be, Gordon, who had been an agricultural student in Scotland. We set off to start up a pineapple plantation in Australia, but decided to get married in San Francisco instead. We came back to Sussex, bought an old Victorian pile and converted it into a hotel. Our combined Scottish and Italian work ethic soon got things going. A restaurant we took on did good business too. The combination of rock music and lasagne went down well with the locals.

But we began to get tired of the hotel and restaurant business after a while. What with two children and the work till midnight, it became exhausting. Gordon decided that he wanted to ride a horse across the South American desert for a year, and I thought I'd do something with more regular hours, like open a shop. Then a whole lot of threads came together, all at once.

I'd been over to the States for a short while and noticed all over the country car repair places called 'Body Shop'. The name struck me as odd. Then I remembered, after returning from America, going into a greengrocer, a sweet shop, a department store: I could get a choice of quantity of apples, of vegetables, confectionery, and so on, but not of skin lotions, or cosmetics. Wouldn't it be lovely, I thought to myself, if I could go into a place, without feeling intimidated, and get something, in whatever size I wanted, for my skin. I remembered the women in Morocco and Tahiti and the natural ingredients they used, and planned on opening our first shop.

All the success that we subsequently reaped stemmed from the same source. We had no money. I had gone to the bank bursting with enthusiasm. But the manager obviously wasn't impressed by this fresh faced young women in jeans, carrying a baby on her back. They turned down my request for a loan. Eventually we raised £4000, but that was hardly anything. So the ideas of re-fill containers, no packaging and subsequently franchising, arose because we had virtually no finance. Had I been given £30 000 I'd probably have sought advice of some design and packaging consultants, and come up with the usual sort of thing. When you don't know about something you get frightened, and you listen to business advice, even if it goes against your social principles.

Anyway, I opened this first 'Body Shop' in Brighton. The name was evocative, quite risqué in the early seventies. We set up shop next to a funeral parlour and had the solicitors after us forthwith. That got into the Press and gave us some good PR. But it wasn't easy to start with. Gordon took off on his desert trip and didn't come back till his horse fell off a cliff. By then I'd opened a second shop, and people were clamouring for new shops.

I knew exactly the ingredients I wanted to develop for my range, but knew nothing about how to make them up. I tried all the big contract manufacturers and supply houses of cosmetics, and they weren't in the slightest interested. I went to them saying, 'I've got this wonderful idea, can I have two gallons of lotion with cocoa butter in it? Just as it is please, no packaging.' Of course they weren't interested. Packaging is where they make all their money. So I had to do it myself.

In fact the greatest buzz for me has been developing new products. But, then having been rejected by the majors, I had to find someone to make them. Not knowing where else to go I looked for a herbal cosmeticist locally. I found one, in the area, willing to make what I wanted. I was over the moon. And then I came across my protégé. A young herbalist rang up after he'd heard about me. He is, like me, a committed ecologist. He's produced some incredible stuff for me over the years. It's fun. Such fun.

The timing of everything, when we started in March 1976, was perfect. Many people had become frightened by recent chemical scare stories. There was a great swing towards health foods, and people were beginning to become more concerned about the environment. The development of jojoba plant-based products, for example, was in direct response to calls to save the endangered sperm whale. All our early recipes were natural and earthy including seaweed, nettles, orchids, henna and so on. People came back again and again. Our shops are like a cross between a chemistry set and a toy shop. You can try anything, mix your own perfumes, play around and have fun.

When Gordon came back, after I had opened our second shop, we decided to go into franchising. Potential franchisees were queuing at the door. In any case, we didn't have the money to finance ourselves. To open up a shop in a prime site on the high street now will cost you £80 000. That's a huge bite into your resources. Franchising is also a fantastic motivator. In retailing the biggest problem is staff. Yet when people run their own business they discover hitherto untapped energies.

We now have 54 franchised outlets in Britain, and 56 abroad. Girls who started here as assistants, or on the stalls in Camden market, now have their own business, turning over a million pounds a year. To see it now is my pat on the back. When, in 1984, we got our placing on the Unlisted Security Market, people expected us to feel an incredible achievement. Certainly we felt, by then, that we have made it financially. But I get my real sense of achievement out of seeing these women running their own successful businesses. It's easy for people who have the money, but a lot of our women started with as little as I did. In the old days it was very inexpensive to buy in. And even today we have a system where the bank guarantees 50 per cent of the start-up capital.

Only 7 of our 110 shops are owned by us. Out most popular locations abroad are Canada, Finland and Sweden. We produce something like 300 different products, notably hair shampoos, hair conditioners, skin creams, cleansers, oils, lotions, soaps, and perfumes. We are essentially in the business of skin and hair care. Our target market is women of 18–35, but the range is expanding all the time. None of our creams is priced at more that £3.00, so we are accessible to all. I look after product development, shop design, publicity, marketing and staff, while Gordon looks after the finance and administration. Out turnover is currently running at about £5 million, with an anticipated pre-tax profit of nearly £1 million.

As far as the cosmetics industry is concerned, we have broken just about every rule in the book. We've never marketed hope. We've never packaged. We never advertised. We're not controlled by design groups. We're the only company who offer six sizes of one product, who refills, the only ones who offer a choice of mud, herbal and conventional shampoos.

Our herbalist will come out of the laboratories to talk to the customers and the assistants are trained on how the products are made and on their suitability for the individual's needs. I continue to develop new products via my travels to overseas countries. Wherever I go I do a lecture on cosmetics, in a hall, or in the marketplace. I then turn the talk inside out and get information from my audience. I find out about their birth and death rituals. Extraordinary folkloric information. They fill in questionnaires for me on how their mothers or grandmothers wash their hair, and that kind of thing. I look for old recipes, and then go to Kew, or write to their university, to find out more about them. I get more detail on a particular material or crop. That way we amass an amazingly comprehensive collection of indigenous recipes. Often I get them substantiated by scientific data, because that's what some people want.

A year ago I wrote to Quaker Oats in Chicago. We use lots of oats in our products. I asked them whether they have developed cosmetic uses for oatmeal. They sent me information on Oatpro, a by-product of theirs, which can be used for eye make up. We've now converted it into liquid foundation. It spurred me on to writing to the Milk Marketing Board. There are these milk mountains, and people want milk baths. But the Board came up with nothing, so we'll have to develop a product ourselves.

Aside from developing new products, I've always enjoyed the momentum of the High Street. There's a constant coming and going. You cannot stand still. The basic house in which you accommodate your product changes. The products don't. I love that change area. There's a buzz. I also love knowing that we have unique and individual strengths. Who else has a perfume bar where you can try things out, and even mix your own products? I've learnt a lot about window display, and we're improving all the time. It's also important to educate your customers, in one or two sentences!

We'll always be adding new products. The problem is deciding which ones to drop. We're influenced by current developments. Our most famous peppermint foot lotion was produced after meeting sponsors of the London Marathon who expressed a hope that something could be formulated for bruised, sweating and aching feet! The elderflower eye gel was a direct response to pleas from girls operating computer terminals who were suffering from eye strain. But we draw a line at anything that doesn't involve skin or hair care. After all, we're so good at what we're doing, why should we go elsewhere? We're not tempted to diversify.

But we're going to open many more shops. We control them extremely well. There's going to be incredible growth in Europe. Germany is bizarre! It's absolutely biting. That's going to be a huge market. We should have 30–40 shops in Scandinavia over the next two years. Once we have 20 shops in a country we contract out the manufacturing. At the moment most of the manufacture of our products in England is also sub-contracted out.

The other thing we want to do in the near future is to establish a training school. Our sales are only as good as our girls. We're converting part of our Marlborough Road store into a training establishment, where we'll bring in lecturers on merchandising and motivation, as well as top herbalists, masseurs and make-up artists. You sell by having the knowledge. If it works we'll want to open the place up to the schools.

At the moment, we are in the process of producing for schools, an information project pack on the cosmetics industry – exploding the myths, current and historical data, employment in the industry, opening areas for class discussion, all aspects of this vibrant industry. When that pack and 'The Body Shop Book' are completed we'll really have something!

Finally there's the proposed massage school. I believe absolutely in the healing power of touch. Massage is the one way you can instantly relieve stress. They should be using it in mental institutions and hospitals.

I opened up as an alternative business. The wealthy have choice, but other people often don't. I like to think of my customers as if they were one-parent families. Those are the people we opened our shop for. Now that we have gained financial security, we want to give something back to society.

Source: Lessem, R. (1987) Interview, in Henry, J. and Walker, D. (eds) *Managing Innovation* (1991), London, Sage Publications, pp.166–170 (adapted from R. Lessem (1987) *Intrapreneurship*, Aldershot, Gower, pp. 148–154)

3.2 Successful versus effective real managers

Fred Luthans

What do *successful* managers – those who have been promoted relatively quickly – have in common with effective managers – those who have satisfied, committed subordinates and high performing units? Surprisingly, the answer seems to be that they have little in common. Successful managers in what we define as 'real organizations' – large and small mainstream organizations, mostly in the mushrooming service industry in middle America – are not engaged in the same day-to-day activities as effective managers in these organizations. This is probably the most important, and certainly the most intriguing, finding of a comprehensive four-year observational study of managerial work that is reported in a recent book by myself and two colleagues, titled *Real Managers*.[1]

The startling finding that there is a difference between successful and effective managers may merely confirm for many cynics and 'passed over' managers something they have suspected for years. They believe that although managers who are successful (that is, rapidly promoted) may be astute politicians, they are not necessarily effective. Indeed, the so-called successful managers may be the ones who do not in fact take care of people and get high performance from their units.

Could this finding explain some of the performance problems facing American organizations today? Could it be that the successful managers, the politically savvy ones who are being rapidly promoted into responsible positions, may not be the effective managers, the ones with satisfied, committed subordinates turning out quantity and quality performance in their units?

This article explores the heretofore assumed equivalence of 'successful managers' and 'effective managers'. Instead of looking for sophisticated technical or governmental approaches to the performance problems facing today's organizations, the solution may be as simple as promoting effective managers and learning how they carry out their jobs. Maybe it is time to turn to the real managers themselves for some answers.

And who are these managers? They are found at all levels and in all types of organizations with titles such as department head, general manager, store manager, marketing manager, office manager, agency chief, or district manager. In other words, maybe the answers to the performance problems facing organizations today can be found in their own backyards, in the managers themselves in their day-to-day activities.

The current view of managerial work

Through the years management has been defined as the famous French administrator and writer Henri Fayol said, by the functions of planning, organizing, commanding, co-ordinating, and controlling. Only recently has this classical view of managers been challenged.[2] Starting with the landmark work of Henry Mintzberg, observational studies of managerial work have found that the normative functions do not hold up. Mintzberg charged that Fayol and others' classical view of what managers do was merely 'folklore'.[3]

On the basis of his observations of five CEOs and their mail, Mintzberg concluded that the manager's job consisted of many brief and disjointed episodes with people inside and outside the organization. He discounted notions such as reflective planning. Instead of the five Fayolian functions of management, Mintzberg portrayed managers in terms of a typology of roles. He formulated three interpersonal roles (figurehead, leader, and liaison); three informational roles (monitor or nerve centre, disseminator, and spokesman); and four decision-making roles (entrepreneur, disturbance handler, resource allocator, and negotiator). Although Mintzberg based this view by managers on only the five managers he observed and his search of the literature, he did ask, and at least gave the beginning of an answer to, the question of what managers really do.

The best known other modern view of managerial work is provided by John Kotter. His description of managers is based on his study of 15 successful general managers. Like Mintzberg, Kotter challenged the traditional view by concluding that managers do not simply perform the Fayolian functions, but rather spend most of their time interacting with others. In particular, he found his general managers spent considerable time in meetings getting and giving information. Kotter refers to these get-togethers as 'network building' Networking accomplishes what Kotter calls a manager's 'agenda' – the loosely connected goals and plans addressing the manager's responsibilities. By obtaining relevant and needed information from his or her networks, the effective general manager is able to implement his or her agenda. Like Mintzberg, Kotter's conclusions are based on managerial work from a small sample of elite managers. Nevertheless, his work represents a progressive step in answering the question of what managers do.

Determining what real managers do

The next step in discovering the true nature of managerial work called for a larger sample that would allow more meaningful generalizations. With a grant from the Office of Naval Research, we embarked on such an effort.[4]

We used trained observers to freely observe and record in detail the behaviours and activities of 44 'real' managers.[5] Unlike Mintzberg's and Kotter's managers, these managers came from all levels and many types of organizations (mostly in the service sector – such as retail stores, hospitals, corporate headquarters, a railroad, government agencies, insurance companies, a newspaper office, financial institutions, and a few manufacturing companies).

We reduced the voluminous data gathered from the free observation logs into managerial activity categories using the Delphi technique. Delphi was developed and used during the heyday of Rand Corporation's 'Think Tank'. A panel offers independent input and then the panel members are given composite feedback. After several iterations of this process, the data were reduced into the 12 descriptive behavioural categories shown in Exhibit 1. These empirically derived behavioural descriptors were then conceptually collapsed into the four managerial activities of real managers:

Descriptive categories derived from free observation	Real managers' activities
Exchanging information Paperwork	Communication
Planning Decision-making Controlling	Traditional management
Interacting with outsiders Socializing/Politicking	Networking
Motivating/Reinforcing Disciplining/Punishing Managing conflict Staffing Training/Developing	Human Resource Management

Exhibit 1   *The activities of real managers*

1   *Communication.* This activity consists of exchanging routine information and processing paperwork. Its observed behaviours include answering procedural questions, receiving and disseminating requested information, conveying the results of meetings, giving or receiving routine information over the phone, processing mail, reading reports, writing reports/memos/letters, routine financial reporting and book-keeping, and general desk work.

2   *Traditional management.* This activity consists of planning, decision making and controlling. Its observed behaviours include setting goals and objectives, defining tasks needed to accomplish goals, scheduling employees, assigning tasks, providing routine instructions, defining problems, handling day-to-day operational crises, deciding what to do, developing new procedures, inspecting work, walking around inspecting the work,

monitoring performance data, and doing preventive maintenance.

3 *Human resource management.* This activity contains the most behavioural categories: motivating/reinforcing, disciplining/ punishing, managing conflict, staffing, and training/developing. The disciplining/punishing category was subsequently dropped from the analysis because it was not generally permitted to be observed. The observed behaviours for this activity include allocating formal rewards, asking for input, conveying appreciation, giving credit where due, listening to suggestions, giving positive feedback, group support, resolving conflict between subordinates, appealing to higher authorities or third parties to resolve a dispute, developing job descriptions, reviewing applications, interviewing applicants, filling in where needed, orienting employees, arranging for training, clarifying roles, coaching, mentoring, and walking subordinates through a task.

4 *Networking.* This activity consists of socializing/politicking and interacting with outsiders. The observed behaviours associated with this activity include non-work-related 'chit chat'; informal joking around; discussing rumours, hearsay and the grapevine; complaining, griping, and putting others down; politicking and gamesmanship; dealing with customers, suppliers, and vendors; attending external meetings; and doing/attending community service events.

These four activities are what real managers do. They include some of the classic notions of Fayol (the traditional management activities) as well as the more recent views of Mintzberg (the communication activities) and Kotter (the networking activities). As a whole, however, especially with the inclusion of human resource management activities, this view of real managers' activities is more comprehensive than previous sets of managerial work.

After the nature of managerial activity was determined through the free observation of the 44 managers, the next phase of the study was to document the relative frequency of these activities. Data on another set of 248 real managers (not the 44 used in the initial portion of this study) were gathered. Trained participation observers filled out a checklist based on the managerial activities at a random time once every hour over a two-week period. We found that the real managers spend not quite a third of their time and effort in communication activities, about a third in traditional management activities, a fifth in human resource management activities, and about a fifth in networking activities. This relative frequency analysis based on observational data of a large sample provides a more definitive answer to the question of what real managers do than the normative classical functions and the limited sample of elite managers used by Mintzberg and Kotter.

How the difference between successful and effective real managers was determined

Discovering the true nature of managerial work by exploding some of the myths of the past and extending the work of Mintzberg and Kotter undoubtedly contributes to our knowledge of management. However, of more critical importance in trying to understand and find solutions to our current performance problems is singling out successful and effective managers to see what they really do in their day-to-day activities. The successful-versus-effective phase of our real managers study consisted of analyzing the existing data based on the frequencies of the observed activities of the real managers. We did not start off with any preconceived notions or hypotheses concerning the relationships between successful and effective managers. In fact, making such a distinction seemed like 'splitting hairs' because the two words are so often used interchangeably. Nevertheless, we decided to define success operationally in terms of the speed of promotion within an organization. We determined a success index on a sample of the real managers in our study. It was calculated by dividing a manager's level in his or her organization by his or her tenure (length of service) there.[6] Thus, a manager at the fourth level of management, who has been with his or her organization for five years, would be rated more successful than a manager at the third level who has been there for 25 years. Obviously, there are some potential problems with such a measure of success, but for our large sample of managers this was an objective measure that could be obtained.

The definition and measurement of effectiveness is even more elusive. The vast literature on managerial effectiveness offered little agreement on criteria or measures. To overcome as many of the obstacles and disagreements as possible, we used a combined effectiveness index for a sample of the real managers in our study that represented the two major – and generally agreed upon – criteria of both management theory/research and practice: (1) getting the job done through high quantity and quality standards of performance, and (2) getting the job done through *people*, which requires their satisfaction and commitment.[7]

We obviously would have liked to use 'hard measures' of effectiveness such as profits and quantity/quality of output or service, but again, because we were working with large samples of real managers from widely diverse jobs and organizations, this was not possible.

What do successful real managers do?

To answer the question of what successful real managers do, we conducted several types of analyses – statistical (using multiple regression techniques), simple descriptive comparisons (for example, top third of managers as measured by the success index vs. bottom third), and relative strength of correctional relationships.[8] In all of these analyses, the importance that networking played in real manager success was very apparent. Of the four real manager activities, only networking had a statistically significant relationship with success. In the comparative analysis we found that the most successful (top third) real managers were doing considerably more networking and slightly more routine communication than their least successful (bottom third) counterparts. From the relative strength of relationship analysis we found that networking makes the biggest relative contribution to manager success and, importantly, human resource management activities make the least relative contribution.

What does this mean? It means that in this study of real managers, using speed of promotion as the measure of success, it was found that successful real managers spent relatively more time and effort socializing, politicking and interacting with outsiders than did their less successful counterparts. Perhaps equally important, the successful real managers did not give much time or attention to the traditional management activities of planning, decision making, and controlling or to the human resource management activities of motivating/reinforcing, staffing, training/developing, and managing conflict. A representative example of this profile would be the following manager's prescription for success:

> *I find that the way to get ahead around here is to be friendly with the right people, both inside and outside the firm. They get tired of always talking shop, so I find a common interest – with some it's sports, with others it's our kids – and interact with them on that level. The other formal stuff around the office is important but I really work at this informal side and have found it pays off when promotion time rolls around.*

In other words, for this manager and for a significant number of those real managers we studied, networking seems to be the key to success.

What do effective real managers do?

Once we answered the question of what successful managers do, we turned to the even more important question of what effective managers do. It should be emphasized once again that, in gathering our observational data for the study, we made no assumptions that the successful real managers were (or were not) the effective managers. Our participant observers were blind to the research questions and we had no hypothesis concerning the relationship between successful and effective managers.

We used the relative strength of correlational relationship between the real managers' effectiveness index and their directly observed day-to-day activities and found that communication and human resource management activities made by far the largest relative contribution to real managers' effectiveness and that traditional management and – especially – networking made by far the least relative contribution.[9]

These results mean that if effectiveness is defined as the perceived quantity and quality of the performance of a manager's unit and his or her subordinates' satisfaction and commitment, then the biggest relative contribution to real manager effectiveness comes from the human oriented activities – communication and human resource management. A representative example of this effectiveness profile is found in the following manager's comments:

> Both how much and how well things get done around here, as well as keeping my people loyal and happy, has to do with keeping them informed and involved. If I make a change in procedure or the guys upstairs give us a new process or piece of equipment to work with, I get my people's input and give them the full story before I lay it on them. Then I make sure they have the proper training and give them feedback on how they are doing. When they screw up, I let them know it, but when they do a good job, I let them know about that too.

This manager, like our study of real managers in general, found that the biggest contribution to effectiveness came from communicating and human resource management activities.

Equally important, however, was the finding that the least relative contribution to real managers' effectiveness came from the networking activity. This, of course, is in stark contrast to our results of the successful real manager analysis. Networking activity had by far the strongest relative relationship to success, but the weakest with effectiveness. On the other hand, human resource management activity had a strong relationship to effectiveness (second only to communication activity), but had the weakest relative relationship to success. In other words, the successful real managers do not do the same activities as the effective real managers (in fact, they do almost the opposite). These contrasting profiles may have significant implications for understanding the current performance problems facing American organizations. However, before we look at these implications and suggest some solutions, let's take a look at those real managers who are both successful *and* effective.

What do managers who are both successful and effective do?

The most obvious concluding question is what those who were found to be both successful and effective really do. This 'combination' real manager, of course, is the ideal – and has been *assumed* to exist in American management over the years.

Since there was such a difference between successful and effective managers in our study, we naturally found relatively few (less than 10% of our sample) that were both among the top third of successful managers and the top third of effective managers. Not surprisingly, upon examining this special group, we found that their activities were very similar to real managers as a whole. They were not like either the successful or effective real managers. Rather, it seems that real managers who are both successful and effective use a fairly balanced approach in terms of their activities. In other words, real managers who can strike the delicate balance between all four managerial activities may be able to get ahead as well as get the job done.

Important is the fact that we found so few real managers that were both successful and effective. This supports our findings on the difference between successful and effective real managers, but limits any generalizations that can be made about successful and effective managers. It seems that more important in explaining our organizations' present performance problems, and what to do about them, are the implications of the wide disparity between successful and effective real managers.

Implications of the successful versus effective real managers findings

If, as our study indicates, there is indeed a difference between successful and effective real managers, what does it mean and what should we do about it? First of all, we need to pay more attention to formal reward systems to ensure that effective managers are promoted. Second, we must learn how effective managers do their day-to-day jobs.

The traditional assumption holds that promotions are based on performance. This is what the formal personnel policies say, this is what new management trainees are told, and this is what every management textbook states *should* happen. On the other hand, more 'hardened' (or perhaps more realistic) members and observers of *real* organizations (not textbook organizations or those featured in the latest best sellers or videotapes) have long suspected that social and political skills are the real key to getting ahead, to being *successful*. Our study lends support to the latter view.

The solution is obvious, but may be virtually impossible to implement, at least in the short run. Tying formal rewards – and especially promotions – to performance is a must if organizations are going to move ahead and become more productive. At a minimum, and most pragmatically in the short run, organizations must move to a performance-based appraisal system. Managers that are *effective* should be *promoted*. In the long run, organizations must develop cultural values that support and reward effective performance, not just successful socializing and politicking. This goes hand-in-hand with the current attention given to corporate culture and how to change it. An appropriate goal for cultural change in today's organizations might simply be to make effective managers successful.

Besides the implications for performance-based appraisals and organizational culture that came out of the findings of our study is a lesson that we can learn from the effective real managers themselves. This lesson is the importance they give and effort they devote to the human-oriented activities of communicating and human resource management. How human resources are managed – keeping them informed, communicating with them, paying attention to them, reinforcing them, resolving their conflicts, training/developing them – all contribute directly to managerial effectiveness.

The disparity our study found between successful and effective real managers has important implications for the performance problems facing today's organizations. While we must move ahead on all fronts in our search for solutions to these problems, we believe the activities basic to the effective real managers in our study – communication and human resource management – deserve special attention.

Endnotes

1   The full reference for the book is Fred Luthans, Richard M. Hodgetts, and Stuart Rosenkrantz, *Real Managers*, Cambridge, MA: Ballinger, 1988. Some of the preliminary material from the real managers study was also included in the presidential speech given by Fred Luthans at the 1986 Academy of Management meeting. Appreciation is extended to the co-authors of the book, Stu Rosenkrantz and Dick Hodgetts, to Diane Lee Lockwood on the first phase of the study, and to Avis Johnson, Hank Hennessey and Lew Taylor on later phases. These individuals, especially Stu Rosenkrantz, contributed ideas and work on the backup for this article.

2   The two most widely recognized challenges to the traditional view of management have come from Henry Mintzberg, *The Nature of Managerial Work*, New York: Harper & Row, 1973; and John Kotter, *The General Managers*, New York: Free Press, 1982. In addition, two recent comprehensive reviews of the nature of managerial work can be found in the following references: Colin P. Hales, 'What do Managers Do? A Critical Review of the Evidence', *Journal of Management Studies*, 1986, 23, pp. 88–115; and Stephen J. Carroll and Dennis J. Gillen, 'Are the Classical Management Functions Useful in Describing Managerial Work?', *Academy of Management Review*, 1987, 12, pp. 38–51.

3   See Henry Mintzberg's article, 'The Manager's Job: Folklore and Fact', *Harvard Business Review*, July–August 1975, 53, pp. 49–61.

4   For those interested in the specific details of the background study, see Luthans, Hodgetts and Rosenkrantz (Endnote 1 above).

5   The source that details the derivation, training of observers, procedures, and reliability and validity analysis of the observation system used in the real managers study in Fred Luthans and Diane L. Lockwood's 'Toward an Observation System for Measuring Leader Behaviour in Natural Settings' in J. Hunt, D. Hosking, C. Schriesheim, and R. Stewart (Eds.) *Leaders and Managers: International Perspectives of Managerial Behaviour and Leadership*, New York: Pergamon Press, 1984, pp. 117–141.

6   For more background on the success portion of the study and the formula used to calculate the success index see Fred Luthans, Stuart Rosenkrantz, and Harry Hennessey, 'What Do Successful Managers Really Do? An Observational Study of Managerial Activities', *Journal of Applied Behavioural Science*, 1985, 21, pp. 255–270.

7   The questionnaire used to measure the real managers, unit quantity and quality of performance was drawn from Paul E. Mott's *The Characteristics of Effective Organizations*, New York: Harper & Row, 1972. Subordinate satisfaction was measured by the Job Diagnostic Index found in P. C. Smith, L. M. Kendall, and C. L. Hulin's *The Measurement of Satisfaction in Work and Retirement*, Chicago: Rand-McNally, 1969. Subordinate commitment is measured by the questionnaire in Richard T. Mowday, L. W. Porter and Richard M. Steers' *Employee–Organizational Linkages: The Psychology of Commitment, Absenteeism, and Turnover*, New York: Academic Press, 1982. These three standardized questionnaires are widely used research instruments with considerable psychometric back-up and high reliability in the sample used in our study.

8   For the details of the multiple regression analysis and simple descriptive comparisons of successful versus unsuccessful managers, see Endnote 6 above. To determine the relative contribution the activities identified in Exhibit 1 made to success, we calculated the mean of the squared correlations (to approximate variance explained) between the observed activities of the real managers and the success index calculated for each target manager. These correlation squared means were then rank ordered to obtain the relative strengths of the managerial activities' contribution to success.

9   The calculation for the relative contribution the activities made to effectiveness was done as described for success in Endnote 8. The statistical and top third–bottom third comparison that was done in the success analysis was not done in the effectiveness analysis. For comparison of successful managers and effective managers, the relative strength of relationship was used; see *Real Managers* (Endnote 1 above) for details.

Source: *Academy of Management Executive*, 1988, Vol. 2, No. 2

3.3 Significance of the political environment

Harold Carter

How politics impacts on businesses

Businesses and non-profit organizations exist in a universe profoundly shaped by governmental rules about what they can and cannot do. This is so from the simplest cafe serving food (and subject to inspection) to nationalised industries (subject to government supervision).

Government as regulator

All businesses are affected by the rules about what does and does not constitute legitimate competitive behaviour. These rules can be explicit – such as the regulations governing monopoly and competition. Equally important, however, are informal rules of the game; what is normal in one country, or at one time in history, may be seen as highly unethical in other countries or at other times. Only recently has bribing politicians been made illegal in the UK. Attitudes to the payment of commission to intermediaries vary significantly between countries – some regarding this as corrupt, others as a normal way to do business. Rules and expectations can change in quite a short time and these changes can profoundly shape the competitive advantage or disadvantage of particular organizations.

In many countries governments also issue specific permissions or refusals for particular types of economic activity to take place, and to take place in specific locations. An obvious example in the UK is the issue of town and country planning, which affects the fundamental competitive structure in areas as diverse as retailing, agriculture and, of course, property development. Governments routinely also intervene directly in other ways – by the imposition of price and wage controls, by credit rationing, by differential taxation (notoriously favouring investment in housing in the UK), or by direction of investment and the formation of national plans (as seen in some form in France, Japan, and even – in earlier decades – the UK).

Pressure groups

Another reason why businesses cannot avoid politics is that they have to deal with people or organizations in the external environment who are neither government, customers, suppliers nor competitors. These groups often have power which they can bring to bear on the organization and its actions. To achieve any given objectives, managers may have to turn these external power structures to their advantage, or work out how to circumvent them.

The most obvious example is the case of pressure groups. But there are many less obvious examples of external power which are sometimes significantly more powerful than pressure groups. External bodies such as media organizations which can influence public taste or morals can powerfully affect the relative competitive position of different organizations. Social groups with power and influence can use those resources to promote activity which enhances their power, or inhibit activity which challenges it. Alliances between powerful social groupings and major economic actors can produce a very uneven playing field for other organizations which are not part of the charmed circle.

Overseas risk assessment

Yet another reason why businesses cannot avoid politics is that many act outside their country of origin, either as exporters or via subsidiaries. This demands risk assessment. Successful strategic management depends on achieving the optimum balance of risks and rewards, generating sustainable competitive advantage either through better risk decisions (things which seemed more risky to others than they turned out to be in the hands of the successful manager), or through superior ability to generate surplus value from more efficient use of resources at any given level of risk.

In practical terms, the first of these means taking risks which others would not. Partly this is a matter of commercial decision-making: is it a viable project? But often it is a matter of political risk as well – for example, banks generating superior returns on assets in the 1970s by lending at higher margins to developing countries; insurance underwriters at Lloyds covering the long-term product liability risks for US asbestosis claims which other insurers would not because they feared the essentially political growth of consumerism and the trends in US court judgements; overseas companies investing in the UK since the 1980s because of a perception that the government had reduced strikes and inflation.

It is easier to find examples of these decisions going wrong (as with Third World debt and asbestosis) than of their going right; the bad decisions are the ones you notice. But even a catalogue of bad decisions is enough to make the point: an attitude to country risk must form an essential part of the strategic decision-making process for all large companies and most small companies today. Even ignoring the more dramatic issues of war, revolution and debt repudiation, politically generated economic growth or recession makes a great difference to the attractiveness of making an effort to develop a given overseas market.

Government as economic actor

Finally businesses cannot avoid politics because in many countries the government itself is a major economic actor, in terms of both infrastructure provision and direct action as a competitor or supplier via nationalised industries. Government is also a very major customer in almost all developed countries, and in some industries (such as aerospace) is often the key customer.

The sale of some state-run enterprises should not disguise the fact that, simply in terms of its purchasing power, the UK public sector still represents by far the largest sector in the domestic UK economy. Local and national government expenditure amounts to 40% of the entire UK Gross Domestic Product. Even after stripping out the effect of transfer payments (e.g. pensions and benefits), direct spending by government on the purchase of goods and services amounts to almost one-quarter of total UK output.[1]

Of course, this economic weight is unevenly distributed in its impact on firms. Some may have government as virtually a sole customer; others may never sell directly to government bodies (though often their customers will do so). But the sheer size of government spending means that purchase decisions by governmental and quasi-governmental bodies can make or break the future of individual firms, and managers would be very foolish to think that they lived in an environment where politics, which often determines the rules governing the behaviour of such bodies, could be ignored. Equally, in other countries the geographical balance of government spending is such that certain regions become even more reliant on the output of the political system than the overall national figures would imply – creating, for example, what is known as 'pork-barrel' politics in many congressional districts in the USA.

When government directly provides services or products, the effect of its economic muscle can be even more marked. For many years, governments of various political hues insisted that the UK electricity generating industry (which they owned) purchase coal from the UK mining industry (which they owned), at way above the prevailing world price. Because of the monopoly position enjoyed by government as electricity supplier, consumers had no choice but to pay whatever price the utilities charged for energy. Thus a major component of the basic costs of many British industries was determined by the fact they were compelled to pay whatever price was necessary to allow the effective cross-subsidisation of industries within the portfolio of industrial investments held by the government. More recently, of course, the decision was taken to privatise both; with the result that the coal industry more or less disappeared overnight. The merits or demerits of successive government policies are not at issue here; the point is that the environment in which managers both inside and outside the energy industry had to operate was shaped by the direct exercise of political control.

Value of political involvement

Our aim here is not to judge the correctness of such actions; rather, it is to show that faced with the impact of government, it would be foolish indeed for any manager to say, 'Politics is nothing to do with me.' Why then do some managers continue to insist that their job is not involved with politics? One explanation may well be that, like the weather, politics is something managers feel they can do little or nothing about. It may be that they recognise the impact of politics,

[1]*Social Trends* 19 (HMSO, 1989), Fig. 6.16, p. 111.

but choose to focus attention on those factors more readily within their grasp.

Is this sensible? Farmers cannot control the weather, but they know what seasons to plant in, and they choose plant species which can survive the expected variations in climate. This involves their studying the weather, thinking carefully about plant strains (there will usually be a trade-off between yield and hardiness), and getting their timing right. Similarly, although managers may not be able to control political events, they may be able to optimise the strategic positioning of their organization by taking specific account of them, and designing their actions accordingly.

In addition, it is sometimes possible to change political constraints. This may be by argument: government can act rationally and change its decisions in response to a coherent case. But individual firms and organizations can affect local and national government in other ways – by lobbying or by bringing sufficient political pressure to bear. And in terms of dealing with pressure group politics, the manager in a typical medium or large organization will often have political power of his or her own, and may be able to overwhelm challengers from pressure groups with superior organization and resources. How far it is morally right to deploy these tools will depend on the merits of any particular situation, but the potential for political action exists.

Even if an issue is too big for an individual organization to affect the outcome, it will often be the case that a group of organizations can put forward a case which will do so. Indeed, as we shall see, government often welcomes such input since it feels it is deprived of contact with the outside world. Examples of this are legion: lawyers protested and secured a change in the 1989 Finance Act, which would otherwise have made discretionary wills illegal; UK brewers have protested vigorously and largely successfully about government proposals to strip them of many of their tied pubs; gun manufacturers in the USA have consistently and successfully opposed measures to introduce gun control; French construction companies are said to have had a major influence on the development of French foreign policy to the Arab world in the 1970s. In the case of direct inward investment, with different national governments making competing bids to attract US and Japanese companies, the abilities of large companies to influence national political decisions have been amply demonstrated.

Source: *B885 The Challenge of the External Environment*, Book 2, Economic and Political Factors, Milton Keynes, Open University Business School, Edn 2.1, 1998, pp. 115–118

3.4 Accounting for marketing

Richard M. S. Wilson

> ## Learning objectives
>
> After reading this chapter you should be able to:
>
> - recognize the role of audits in securing control over marketing activities;
> - understand how to set about an audit of marketing, distribution and retailing activities;
> - appreciate the characteristics of an effective audit.

Introduction

Management auditing exists to appraise and review critically the firm's management process, covering the extent and effectiveness of the system of delegation, channels of communication, harmony of coordination, the adequacy of the methods of planning and control, the skill in supplying management information as a guide to action and, in general, the competence of supervisory and specialist teams.

This is a wide range of matters to review and appraise, but at all times the management auditor must bear in mind that he or she is not the manager: his or her function is to supply a service to management, and the auditor can only adequately discharge this service by remaining independent and free of executive responsibility. Nevertheless, it is vital that management auditors adopt a management perspective, lest they become obsessed with the accuracy of figures rather than with the managerial implications of inefficient practices.

A particularly significant development within the field of management auditing is the operational audit. This is totally removed from any financial audit concept, since the procedure is to select an activity for study, review and appraisal. The following are three examples: the marketing audit, the distribution audit and the retail audit.

Audits

The marketing audit

The marketing audit exists to help correct difficulties and to improve conditions that may already be good. While these aims may be achieved by a piece-meal examination of individual activities, they are better achieved by a total programme of evaluation studies. The former approach is termed a 'vertical audit' as it is only concerned with one element of the marketing mix at any one time. In contrast, the second approach, the 'horizontal audit', is concerned with optimizing the use of resources, thereby maximizing the total effectiveness of marketing efforts and outlays. As such, it is by far the more difficult of the two, and hence rarely attempted.

No matter which form of marketing audit is selected, top management (via its audit staff) should ensure that no area of marketing activity goes unevaluated, and that every aspect is evaluated in accordance with standards that are compatible with the overall success of the marketing organization and of the firm as a whole. This, of course, requires that all activities be related to the established hierarchy of objectives.

The auditing process should begin with agreement being reached between the organization's marketing director and the marketing auditor – someone from inside or outside the organization – regarding the specific objectives, the breadth and depth of coverage, the sources of data, the report format and the time period for the audit. Included within this should be a plan of who is to be interviewed and the questions that are to be asked.

With regard to the question of *who* is to be questioned, it needs to be emphasized that the audit should never be restricted to the company's executives; it should also include customers, the dealer network, relevant employees and other outside groups. In this way, a better and more complete picture of the company's position and its effectiveness can be developed. In the case of customers and dealers, for example, the auditor should aim to develop satisfaction ratings that are capable of highlighting areas in need of attention.

Once the information has been collected, the findings and recommendations need to be presented with emphasis being given to the type of action needed to overcome any problems, the time scale over which remedial action is to be taken, and the names of those who are to be responsible for this.

Within the general framework of the external and internal audits, Kotler *et al.* (1989) suggest there are six specific dimensions that are of direct interest to the auditor. These are:

1 The *marketing environment audit*, which involves an analysis of the major macroeconomic forces and trends within the organization's task environment. This includes markets, customers, competitors, distributors, dealers and suppliers.

2 The *marketing strategy audit*, which focuses upon a review of the organization's marketing objectives and strategy, with a view to

determining how well suited they are to the current and forecasted market environment.

3 The *marketing organization audit*, which follows on from the previous aspect and is concerned specifically with an evaluation of the structural capability of the organization and its suitability for implementing the strategy needed for the developing environment.

4 The *marketing systems audit*, which covers the quality of the organization's systems for analysis, planning and control.

5 The *marketing productivity audit*, which examines the profitability of different aspects of the marketing programme and the cost effectiveness of various levels of marketing expenditure.

6 The *marketing functions audit* involving a detailed evaluation of each of the elements of the marketing mix.

The distribution audit

In the planning and control of costs and effectiveness in distribution activities the management audit can be of considerable value. Not surprisingly, however, it entails a complex set of procedures right across the function if it is to be carried out thoroughly. The major components are the channel audit, the physical distribution management (PDM) audit, the competitive audit and the customer service audit. Each of these will be considered briefly in turn.

(a) The channel audit

Channels are made up of the intermediaries (such as wholesalers, factors, retailers) through which goods pass on their route from manufacture to consumption. The key channel decisions include:

- choosing intermediaries;
- determining the implications (from a physical distribution point of view) of alternative channel structures; and
- assessing the available margins.

It follows from the nature of these decisions that the main focus of a channel audit will be on structural factors on the one hand and on cost/margin factors on the other.

(b) The PDM audit

There are three primary elements within this audit: that of company profile (which includes the handling cost characteristics of the product range and the service level that is needed in the light of market conditions); PDM developments (both of a technological and of a contextual nature); and that of the current system's capability.

Cost aspects exist in each of these elements, but operating costs loom largest in the last since it is predominantly concerned with costs and capacity. For example, some of the items that will be subjected to audit will include those shown in Figure 1.

(c) The competitive audit

Through this phase it should be possible to ascertain the quality of competitors' distribution policies, practices and facilities, and especially the level of service that competitors are able to offer (and maintain). Within the competitive audit regard should also be paid to channel structures, pricing and discount policies and market shares.

Capacity utilization	– Warehouse
	– Transportation
	– Flexibility and expansion scope
Warehouse facilities	– Total costs
	– Age and maintenance costs
	– Flexibility throughout/period
	– Total throughout/period
	– Returns handled — number
	— recovery time
	– Picking accuracy
	– Service levels/back orders
	– Cube utilization
	– Cost of cube bought out
Inventory	– Total inventory holding costs
	– Product group costs
	– Service levels — total
	— plant
	— field
	– Field inventory holding costs
	– Transfers — number
	— volume
	– Stockout effects — loss of business
	— rectification costs
Transportation	– Total costs
	– Production to field units
	– Field units to customers
	– Vehicle utilization
	– Vehicle cube utilization
	– Total volumes shipped
	– Cost per mile — volumes shipped
	— cases/pallets shipped
	– Costs of service bought out
	– Costs by mode/comparisons

Communications	– Total costs		
	– Order communication times	– method	
		– cost	
	– Time and costs per line item per order method for:		
	– order processing and registration		
	– credit investigation		
	– invoice and delivery note preparation		
	– statement preparation		
	– Number and cost of customer queries		
	– Salespeople's	– calls/day	
		– calls/territory/day	
		– calls/product group/day	
		– calls/customer group/day	
	– Salespeople's use of time	– selling	
		– inventory checking	
		– merchandising	
		– order progressing	
Unitization	– Total costs		
	– Volumes shipped		
	– Unitization method/proportions of:		
	– pallets		
	– roll pallets		
	– containers		
	– Costs of assembly and handling by load type		
Service achieved (by market segment)	– Total costs		
	– Service levels operated/costs		
	– Delivery times		
	– Delivery reliability		
	– Order processing and progressing		
	– Order picking efficiency		
	– Claims procedure/time/cost		
Volume throughout	– Total throughout	– volume	
		– weight	
		– units	
	– Total costs		
	– Throughput/field locations	– volume	
		– weight	
		– units	
	– Throughput fluctuations		
	– Flexibility (capacity availability/time)		

Figure 1   *System capability factors*

(d)   The customer service audit

Given that the level of service is at the centre of physical distribution management it is essential to monitor regularly its cost and quality characteristics.

A very thorough approach to the distribution audit is that developed at the Cranfield School of Management by Martin Christopher and his colleagues.

The retail audit

As in marketing and distribution, the management audit can be developed to evaluate retail activities. The main steps of a retail audit are shown in Figure 2 These consist of the following:

1   *Determining who is to do the audit.* There are basically three possibilities:

    (a) company specialists (i.e. internal auditors with particular expertise in retail and in the organization in question;

    (b) departmental managers on a do-it-yourself basis; and

    (c) outside specialists on a consulting basis.

    The relative costs, degree of objectivity and expertise, plus the scope for combining 'vertical' audits into a 'horizontal' one will influence the choice.

2   *Determining when and how often the audit is to be conducted.* Various 'obvious' times suggest themselves (see Figure 2). Annual audits are, however, rather too infrequent to be of significant operational benefit.

3   *Determining which areas are to be audited.* In other words, should the audit be specific to one factor ('vertical') or an across-the-board assessment ('horizontal')?

4   *Developing the audit forms.* These detailed questionnaires should cover all the aspects worthy of investigation (given the aims of the audit). Examples will be given later in this section – see Figures 3–5.

5   *Carrying out the audit.* A number of important questions arise in this phase of the audit (as shown in Figure 2).

6   *Reporting to management.* Once the audit has been completed it is essential to present the findings (with appropriate recommendations) to management. It is only as a result of managerial decisions based on a carefully prepared report that action leading to improvements in cost control procedures is likely.

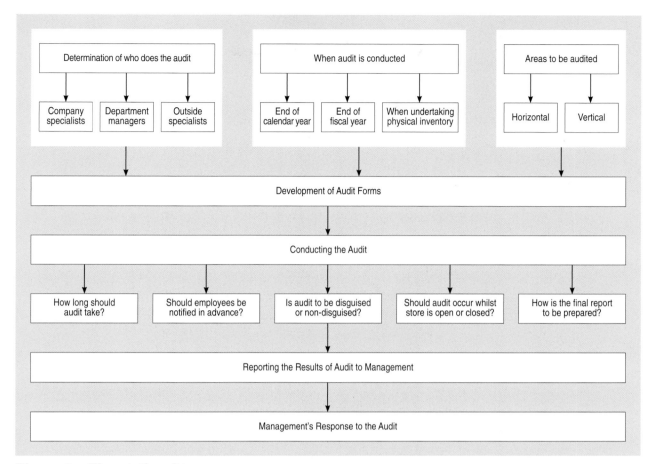

Figure 2 *The retail audit process*

1   Do you express your plans in terms of a budget, covering sales, stocks, mark-ups and expenses?

2   Do you set up your budget for relatively short periods?

3   Do you make an organized effort to determine the potential sales of your merchandise lines in your community and to calculate your market share?

4   In controlling your operations, do you frequently compare actual results with the budget projections you have made; and do you then adjust your merchandising, promotion and expense plans as indicated by deviations from these projections?

5   Do your key employees have a voice in formulating budget plans concerning them?

6   Do you study industry data and compare the results of your operation with them?

7   Do you think in terms of ratios and percentages, rather than exclusively in pounds and pence?

8   Do you use a variety of measures of productivity, such as:

    (a) net profit as percentage of your net worth;

    (b) stockturn (ratio of cost of your sales to the value of your average inventory);

    (c) gross profit margin per pound of cost investment in merchandise (pounds of gross margin divided by your average inventory at cost);

    (d) ales per square metre of space (net sales divided by total number of square metres of space); and

    (e) selling cost per cent for each salesperson (remunerations of the salesperson divided by that person's sales)?

Figure 3   *Management for small retailers: budgetary control and productivity*

1   Does someone other than the cashier or book-keeper open all mail and prepare a record of receipts that will be checked against deposits?

2   Do you deposit all of each day's cash receipts in the bank without delay?

3   Do you restrict the use of your petty cash funds to payment of small expenditures (not exceeding a stated amount) and limit them to the amount needed for a short period of time – a week or two?

4   Do you require adequate identification of 'cash-take' customers who want to pay by cheque and those who ask you to cash cheques?

5   Have you taken adequate steps to protect your cash from robbery?

6   Is your postage metered?

7   Are your cheques prenumbered?

8   Are you careful to lay aside cash for all amounts withheld from employees' wages for taxes, national insurance, etc., and for all VAT collected and to remit these sums as required to the appropriate authorities?

9   Do you calculate your cash flow regularly (monthly, for example) and take steps to provide enough cash for each period's needs?

10 Have you established, in advance, a line of credit at your bank, not only to meet seasonal requirements but also to permit borrowing at any time for emergency needs?

11 Do you consistently avoid drawing cheques to 'cash' and signing blank cheques?

12 Have you taken out indemnity insurance on your cashier and other employees who handle cash and securities?

13 Do you keep company securities under lock and key, preferably in a safe deposit vault?

14 Do you control your liabilities with the same degree of care you devote to your assets?

15 To permit modernization and expansion of your premises (if you rent them), have you seriously considered your landlord as a source for the additional capital you will need?

16 Do you maintain a close personal relationship with your local bank?

Figure 4   *Management for small retailers: cash and finance*

1   Do you have a credit policy?

2   Do you set definite credit limits and explain your rules carefully to all credit applicants?

3   When customers do not make payments as agreed, do you follow up promptly?

4   If you have your own credit plan, do you have a simple method of identifying credit customers and authorizing their purchases?

5   Have you introduced a revolving credit plan whereby customers can complete payment for merchandise by means of a number of monthly, or weekly, payments and are privileged to buy more at any time within a set limit?

6   Are your bad debt losses comparable with those of other similar stores?

7   Periodically, do you review your accounts to determine their status?

8   Are you a member of a retail credit bureau, and do you actively use the information it provides?

Figure 5 *Management for small retailers: credit*

In proceeding through these stages it is inevitable that a number of problems will be met. Not least of all the audit will be expensive, in terms both of money and time, but there are human problems (such as individuals' feeling threatened by investigations) and problems of data availability and accuracy to contend with.

To give a clearer indication of how one might develop a retail audit the questionnaires shown in Figures 3–5 offer suggestions relating to small retailers' activities. Figure 3 focuses on budgetary and productivity issues, Figure 4 on cash and finance, and Figure 5 on credit policies. Similar questionnaires can be developed for customer relations, personnel management, stock control, purchasing, pricing, advertising and promotion, display equipment and layout, and many other aspects of a small retailer's activities. Collectively, a set of questionnaires developed along these lines will facilitate a systematic, horizontal audit.

The specific needs of large retailers will need to be met by questionnaires designed especially to suit their organizational and operational characteristics.

Other examples of operational audits would include the purchasing function, covering the full spectrum of activities and procedures from the time an item is required and ordered until it is finally received, paid for, and charged to expense in the accounts.

The integral aspects of the study would include:

- the factors required for effective purchasing
- cooperation and coordination with other departments
- controls

- purchase authorization
- selection of suppliers
- negotiation of terms
- issue of official purchase orders
- follow-up of order
- receipt and inspection of delivered goods
- stores procedures

Similarly, studies can be done on the efficiency and weaknesses of every function in the company, and should lead to cost savings and profit improvement in all cases.

Although similar to O & M studies in some respects, operational audits are concerned with improvements in managerial processes rather than purely paper flows. They are more comprehensive than other forms of control, but nevertheless are best used as supplementary control devices, and not as primary ones.

As with marketing research and operations research studies, the initial outcome of the management audit is a report. If this is poorly written, or fails to include all pertinent details, it may cause damaging decisions to be made. The need for skill and patience in drawing up reports can hardly be exaggerated, as the overall effectiveness of any study depends mainly upon the report, the distribution it receives, and the effectiveness of the follow-up action.

The characteristics of effective audits

Four dimensions can be highlighted in seeking to characterize an effective audit. These are that it should be comprehensive, systematic, independent and periodic. Let us consider each of these in a little more detail (after Kotler 1988).

(a) Comprehensive

For the auditing process to be worthwhile it is essential that it cover *all* of the major elements of the organization's marketing activities, including those that seemingly are doing well, rather than just a few apparent trouble spots. In this way a distinction can be drawn between the *marketing audit* and a *functional audit* which would focus far more specifically upon a particular element of marketing activity such as sales or pricing. As an example of this, a functional audit might well suggest that a high sales-force turnover and low morale is due to a combination of inadequate sales training and a poor compensation package. A more fundamental reason, however, might be that the company has a poor or inadequate product range and an inappropriate pricing and advertising strategy. It is the comprehensiveness of the marketing audit that is designed to reveal these sorts of factors and to highlight the *fundamental* causes of the organization's problems.

(b) Systematic

In carrying out the audit it is essential that a sequential diagnostic process be adopted covering the three areas to which reference was made earlier: the external environment, internal marketing systems and specific marketing activities. This process of diagnosis is then followed by the development *and implementation* of both short-term and long-term plans designed to correct the weaknesses identified and, in this way, improve upon levels of marketing effectiveness.

(c) Independent

As with a financial audit, there are several ways in which the marketing audit can be conducted. These include:

- a self-audit in which managers use a checklist to assess their own results and methods of operation;
- an audit by a manager of the same status but drawn from a different department or division within the organization;
- an audit by a more senior manager within the same department or division;
- the use of a company auditing office;
- a company task force audit group;
- an audit conducted by an outside specialist.

Of these it is generally recognized that an audit conducted by an outside specialist is likely to prove the most objective and to exhibit the independence that any internal process will almost inevitably lack. Adopting this approach should also ensure that the audit receives the undivided time and attention that is needed. In practice, however, many large companies make use of their own audit teams (something which 3M, for example, has pioneered).

This question of *who* should conduct the audit has been the subject of a considerable amount of research and discussion in recent years with, as indicated above, the argument revolving around the issue of objectivity (in other words, how objective can a line manager be in conducting an evaluation of activities for which he or she has direct responsibility?). It is largely because of this that it has been suggested that outside consultants should be used to ensure impartiality. This is likely to prove expensive if done annually, and the answer is increasingly being seen to lie in a compromise whereby an outside consultant is used every third or fourth year, with line managers from different departments or divisions being used in the intervening periods. Alternatively an organization might opt for what is in essence a composite approach, with an external auditor being used initially to validate line managers' self-audits, and subsequently to integrate them to produce an audit result for the marketing function as a whole.

To a large extent, however, it can be argued that the supposed difficulties of achieving impartiality are overstated since a sufficiently well-structured and institutionalized auditing process can overcome many of these difficulties. There is a need, therefore, for managers to be trained in how best to use auditing procedures and, very importantly, for the audit process to be endorsed by senior management: without top management commitment to the audit process and, in turn, to the need to act on the results that emerge, the entire exercise is likely to prove valueless.

(d) Periodic

If the company is to benefit fully from the auditing process it is essential that it be carried out on a regular basis. All too often in the past companies have been spurred into conducting an audit largely as the result of poor performance. Ironically, this poor performance can often be traced to a myopia on the part of management, stemming from a failure to review activities on a sufficiently regular basis, something that was pointed to by Shuchman (1950), who commented that 'No marketing operation is ever so good that it cannot be improved. Even the best *must* be better, for few if any marketing operations can remain successful over the years by maintaining the status quo.'

Summary

Within this chapter the focus has been on marketing, distribution and retail audits as means to facilitate feedback control.

Management audits in general seek to give a basis for improving performance that may already be good, and can be undertaken in a horizontal (i.e. comprehensive) or vertical (i.e. partial) way. We considered the central features of audits dealing with marketing, distribution and retail activities.

The characteristics of effective audits were identified (i.e. they should be comprehensive, systematic, independent and periodic).

Source: Wilson, R. M. S. (1999) *Accounting for Marketing*, London, International Thomson Business Press, Ch. 9, pp. 118–128

3.5 The Bank of Scotland's COMPASS – The Future of Bank Lending?

Alan Sangster

Pergamon

Expert Systems With Applications, Vol. 9, No. 4, pp. 457–468, 1995
Copyright © 1995 Elsevier Science Ltd
Printed in the USA. All rights reserved
0957-4174/95 $9.50 + .00

0957-4174(95)00016-X

The Bank of Scotland's COMPASS—The Future of Bank Lending?

ALAN SANGSTER

Department of Accountancy (Academic), Aberdeen University, Dunbar Street, Aberdeen AB9 2TY, UK

Abstract—*This paper describes the background surrounding the need for risk analysis of commercial business within the domain of bank lending and of the development of an expert system for that task. Previous attempts at constructing expert systems in this area have either proved unsuccessful, software difficulties often being cited as the cause; or have stopped short of encapsulating all the relevant expertise. This paper considers the relevance of knowledge engineering to successful expert system construction. It reports on the development and structure of COMPASS, the Bank of Scotland's commercial lending adviser expert system which, by appropriate application of knowledge engineering, has succeeded in capturing and modelling the inherent risk of the Bank of Scotland's commercial lending process. The stages of its development are outlined; the knowledge elicitation process is described; knowledge articulation is examined from the perspective of the expert; the architecture of the system is explained; and the consultation procedure is described. In addition, reference is made to major attempts elsewhere to produce lending adviser expert systems; and the advantages; by-products, and long-term benefits of COMPASS are summarized.*

1. INTRODUCTION

Banks which have had successful experiences with the implementation of knowledge-based solutions state that whatever they enacted through AI created an order of magnitude in *difference regarding cost savings*. With such tremendous competitive advantage in their reach, these are going to be the survivor banks. (Chorafas & Steinmann, 1991, p. 17).

EXPERT SYSTEMS HAVE been used in banking for a number of years and across the range of traditional banking activities—personal customer portfolio advising (Feigenbaum, McCorduck, & Nii, 1988, pp. 119–122), fraud detection (Lecot, 1988), credit assessment (Butera, Frascari, & Iacona, 1990), bank liquidity risk (Klein & Methlie, 1990), and natural language interfaces (Harris, 1992). Examples of the application of expert systems technology across the domain are reported by Chorafas and Steinmann (1991).

Not surprisingly, given the importance of risk minimization, it is in the handling of risk, generally through the use of probability analysis on financial data, that most banking expert system development appears to have occurred. However, financial data is not, in itself, sufficient for an assessment of the risk associated with bank lending. Qualitative knowledge (for example, on company structure and management) is required before a "true" assessment can be made. Yet, with some notable exceptions, most bank lending expert systems have tended to emphasize the financial data and its characteristics, leaving the qualitative aspects in the hands of the human experts.

This limitation has been exposed by the large losses on bank lending that have been experienced since the late 1980s. A recent survey that considered these losses (*The Economist*, 1993) highlighted a general failure by banks to address risk effectively; and a misplaced faith in traditional chartist-based financial data analysis that blindly accepted the book value placed on assets, irrespective, for example, of the economic situation or outlook. It also cited examples of increased risks and losses resulting from the failure of banks to apply a defined or consistent lending policy.

The banks have responded to their losses by recognizing the need to proactively address all aspects of risk. They have been developing more sophisticated software to support this revised philosophy (see, for example, Friedman, 1989) and software companies are endeavouring to provide them with generic packages suited to their needs. However, producing software capable of capturing the necessary quantitative *and* qualitative expertise to handle risk in lending has proved difficult and, to-date, no satisfactory generic product has been produced.

Requests for reprints should be sent to Alan Sangster, Department of Accountancy (Academic), Aberdeen University, Dunbar Street, Aberdeen AB9 2TY, UK (e-mail, A. SANGSTER@ABDN.AC.UK).

457

Yet, theoretically, the elicitation of expertise relating to the qualitative aspects should be possible using the same knowledge engineering techniques as are already in use for the capture of expertise concerning financial data and its characteristics. Once elicited, it would be surprising were the software-related issues truly as major as currently appears to be the case. If it is indeed the case that it is a software problem, the expertise has presumably been elicited and then found to be incapable of being encapsulated within an expert system. However, a review of the literature reveals little evidence of this.

Chorafas and Steinmann (1991, p. 24) suggest that there are three reasons why (some) banks are not yet ready for AI:

- the *online capabilities* are substandard because of low network capability
- the *cultural environment* has not yet changed (i.e., not yet accepted the technology)
- the *practical knowhow* in knowledge engineering is non-existent

Applying these suggestions to the problems experienced in the development of lending risk assessment expert systems, the first is not likely to be an issue. It is hardly likely that a bank would be considering a major investment in expert system technology of this type unless it could both distribute it widely through its organization and directly access its own database of customer information. The second may be relevant, but if development has started, non-acceptance of the technology is not a barrier to commencement; rather it is a hurdle that has to be overcome once development has been underway for some time. Successful development should prevent rejection at that stage. The third suggestion appears to be the key. Expertise is marked with individuality (Firlej & Hellens, 1991, p. 1). It represents the sum of experience in a particular task.

… an expert is likely to have well established patterns of thinking that have become submerged by habit. There is no reason for the expert to carry a conscious model of how he or she thinks … yet that is precisely what … [*needs to be known*] … if a successful emulation of the expert's behaviour is to be constructed. (Firlej and Hellens, 1991, pp. 2–3)

Unless someone skilled in knowledge engineering is involved, it may prove impossible to identify the expertise and develop a successful expert system. Even where someone with these skills is available, time must be allowed to enable the deeply submerged expertise to be brought out. If expertise in knowledge engineering is non-existent within the organization (and is not identified and obtained prior to formulating the project) there are a number of reasonably obvious implications. For example, unrealistic timetables will be set; unrealistic expectations will be created; and inappropriate emphasis will be placed on the various stages of the elicitation process. The result would likely be abandonment of the project, a loss of faith in expert systems for the task, and a reversion to traditional human-based approaches.

If the banks do indeed have a scarcity of practical knowledge in knowledge engineering, this would certainly hinder development of expert systems for lending risk assessment. Yet, even if sufficient knowledge engineers were available to enable the appropriate knowledge to be successfully elicited, would it transpire that the commercial loan risk assessment domain is too complex a domain for existing technology? In other words, would it be found to have been a software-related problem after all?

One way to resolve this issue would be to identify a case where a bank had succeeded in capturing the required expertise and was successfully using a loan assessment expert system. Such a finding would support the hypothesis that the explanation for the present lack of lending risk assessment expert systems is due to knowledge engineering-related issues rather than to a lack of appropriate software. This paper reports on the development of such a system.

2. BANK LOAN RISK ASSESSMENT EXPERT SYSTEMS

Hartvigsen (1992) comprehensively argued the need to go beyond data modelling and to address qualitative factors in any loan risk assessment expert system. He reviewed the process of loan authorization and highlighted the dependence placed by lenders upon mathematical bankruptcy prediction models. He also questioned the merits of using these techniques because:

- identified predictors are not stable over time and samples,
- multiple discriminant analysis is too imprecise on the impact of individual variables,
- the operating environment is subject to constant variation,
- geographical factors are frequently overlooked, and
- there is considerable inconsistency between the various models that have been produced.

In addition, he questioned the assumptions made when applying financial ratio analysis. For example, despite a proliferation of accounting standards (which are intended to prescribe action and/or restrict choice in approach), the composition of items in financial statements is still very much a matter of choice for the reporting entity and will depend upon its circumstances at the time. He concluded that there is no overall accepted theory on how to evaluate the results of ratio analysis, never mind the actual ratios to use; and that, as a result, it takes many years of experience to build-up the heuristic knowledge necessary to take ratio results and apply them appropriately in the assessment of a loan application. If risk is to be modelled and incorporated into an expert system, these heuristics must be identified.

Those systems that have been reported as having attempted to address the heuristic-related qualitative aspects have only captured part of the relevant expertise. KABAL (Hartvigsen, 1990, 1992), a bank loan authorization expert system developed with the Norwegian Tromsø Sparebank, performs analysis of financial statements. It also considers guarantees, the market, and the company management/organization. The user is guided through the appraisal. However, there are many points where the user is still required to have relatively deep expertise. For example, when assigning appropriate values to assets. The system can only be described as a preliminary step towards encapsulating the expertise required to truly guide loan officers through the appraisal process.

PARMENIDE (Butera, Frascari, & Iacona, 1990), developed for the Italian Banco di Napoli, reviews loan applications on the basis of its prediction of the future position of the company applying for the loan facility. It produces projected financial statements and cash flows, evaluates the securities offered by the company, assesses the ability of the company to finance and repay the loan requested, and produces a final report recommending appropriate action. During the assessment, the customer is visited in order to assess the working conditions, assets, etc. The management, background of the company, and its market are incorporated into the analysis. Information from external agencies is used in order to incorporate market data.

While PARMENIDE is an example of a move towards the use of qualitative data and related heuristics, much of the analysis requires expertise on the part of the loan officer and it can only handle established companies (due to a need for historical data). It also relies heavily on historical data for future projections, rather than making use of company projections. Finally, while it pays some regard to the market, it does so from a qualitative rather than quantitative perspective. Hence the assessment, to some extent, is made in the absence of detailed knowledge of the sector in which the company operates. Like KABAL, it guides the loan officer through the entire process. However, it requires input of generic risk-related expertise, part of which is provided centrally by the Bank's lending expert, not the loan officer dealing with the application, during the second phase of the assessment.

Both these expert systems demonstrate how it is possible to move beyond the traditional data modelling approach in the assessment of bank loan applications. However, neither of them can or would claim to do more than superficially model the risk inherent in the lending situation. An expert system that does model both the quantitative and the qualitative aspects of the assessment of risk in lending situations is Rackwick's COMPASS, developed for the *Bank of Scotland* and used in the assessment, monitoring, and administration of bank lending to middle-market corporate institutions throughout the UK.

The COMPASS project started in 1987. The first prototype was completed in 1988 and the first fully working system started testing in 1992. Testing was initially by *Bank of Scotland* staff. In 1993, they were augmented by a team of chartered accountants from one of the largest international accountancy firms. By mid-1994, COMPASS was installed in 20% of the *Bank of Scotland*'s corporate branches throughout the UK covering, as a result, 80% of the Bank's corporate lending portfolio. Bank loan officers are required to use the system and such has been its success at enhancing and supporting the management of risk that the $2m it cost to develop had a payback in terms of months rather than years.

The remainder of this paper describes the various stages in the development of COMPASS, its structure, and the benefits derived.

3. THE DEVELOPMENT PROCESS

Initially, there were two people involved in the development process: a psychologist, who performed the role of knowledge engineer; and the Bank's leading lending expert. Once some tangible knowledge had been elicited and the expertise began to crystallize, a programmer was added to the team and over the following years, the programming team grew to its 1995 level of ten. Throughout the development and testing period, there was never more than one expert involved, though, occasionally, a different expert was used in order to incorporate expertise where the principal expert believed the functionality should be expanded.

3.1. Preliminary Activities and Decisions

COMPASS arose from the experiences of the two developers while involved in the mid-80s UK ALVEY Directorate Initiative (Edwards & Connell, 1989, p. 6; Bench-Capon & Rada, 1991). One was part of a team of about 20 involved in attempting to develop an expert system to appraise company financial health. All the participants had their own (often conflicting) ideas and views and the whole venture eventually ended before anything significant could be produced. However, he remained convinced that there was potential for the development of such a system, believing it was the approach, rather than the domain that was at the root of that project's inability to deliver a useful product.

The developer who was involved in that Alvey project was a senior loans officer with the *Bank of Scotland*. Discussing his ideas at length with the other developer of COMPASS, they concluded that by restricting themselves to using a single expert, they could overcome many of the problems of the Alvey project. They believed they could develop a satisfactory lending advisor expert system encapsulating the senior loans officer's expertise in about six man-months—this timescale was based on the senior loans officer's belief concerning the complexity of the domain knowledge.

The other developer had worked previously on medical diagnostic expert systems, but had no expert knowledge of banking or loan authorization.

Their initial and enduring view was that the main lending process occurs away from the financial data—the loan officer should not just look at the balance sheet and wonder about ratios. Rather, the financial data should be analysed and then considered in the context of other factors, including the environment in which the customer operates and the customer's management team.

Three maxims were observed throughout the development of COMPASS—keep it:

SIMPLE (in scope and application),

FLEXIBLE (to allow infinite refinement), *and*

FOCUSED (limited number of experts and limited number of those who were aware of the development).

The two developers started by attempting to derive a conceptual model of the loan authorization process. This was then used to identify the various factors that had to be developed.

3.2. Knowledge Elicitation

According to Firlej and Hellens (1991, pp. 50–81), successful knowledge elicitation

*   requires:
    (1) sound co-operation and mutual understanding between expert and knowledge engineer
    (2) flexibility on the part of the knowledge engineer
    (3) careful verification of information provided by the expert—when appropriate, independent corroboration should be used
    (4) that the expert be kept properly motivated, preferably intrinsically (i.e., as a result of the expert's own internalised reasons or personal interests) rather than extrinsically (i.e., in response to external stimuli)
    (5) patience
    (6) feedback from the expert concerning the manner in which the elicitation is being conducted
*   is enhanced by task analysis (i.e., dividing the task into sub-tasks that can be treated as discrete areas for analysis)
*   may be enhanced through the use of repertory grid techniques (Kelly, 1955; Gaines & Shaw, 1980; Shaw & Gaines, 1983; Turban, 1992)
*   benefits from the knowledge engineer showing an interest in the expert's field

All these factors were present throughout the development of COMPASS.

3.2.1. Overview. COMPASS is continually being updated and extended and the knowledge elicitation process, therefore, is still ongoing in 1995. With respect to the version of COMPASS released to the *Bank of Scotland*'s branches in 1993, knowledge elicitation had taken approximately five years—ten times the period foreseen at the start. An incremental software development approach was adopted (Feigenbaum, McCorduck, & Nii, 1988, p. 45). There were many weeks of discussion before the process developed any structure. Elicitation and development were on a trial-and-error basis that moved from diagrams to computer programs. When ideas crystallized, they were incorporated into the relevant module and the expert was asked to comment on whether the interpretation was correct. The module was modified in the light of his comments and then shown to him again, and so on. Much of the complex knowledge was elicited over a long time and many alterations were made as a result of the expert mulling over a point and allowing his thoughts to crystallize in more detail than previously. For this reason, the length of the elicitation process is viewed by the developers as having been a major advantage.

3.2.2. Detailed. Modularity was adopted from the start. Using a combination of a paper-based repertory grid approach and an in-depth interview approach, each module component was mapped-out on paper and the expert invited to comment on the structure. A process of iterative prototyping on the knowledge elicitation incorporated the developers' resolve to restrict themselves to one logical view of how things were done, use that as a core, and then develop and refine it. The refinement involved the expert in redefining the processes involved and, where available, obtaining the views of other experts on the appropriateness of the statement of expertise. In effect, the expertise was collected at a fairly broad level and then refined and broken-down to generate detail where appropriate.

In assessing a business's viability, at the top level there is an information gathering process, and an analysis process. For all businesses, this top level objective may be broken-down into three sub-areas—their accounts, management, and business. Each of these areas have objectives that must be identified and it must be decided how each of them is to be met—from a company's accounts; from their management; from understanding the business in which they operate. Once identified, these sources of information can then go through the analysis process and become integrated within that sub-area, subsequently to influence the primary objective of assessing the business's viability. During the knowledge elicitation process, this attention to detail could result in an explosion of knowledge, much of which is redundant—effectively, over-engineering would arise and the system could prove impossible to encode. However, this was largely avoided in the knowledge elicitation process adopted for the development of COMPASS through keeping to the axiom of *simplicity*, overlooking, even ignoring stages in the process—effectively, constraints were violated in order to identify the key objectives.

Nevertheless, on occasion, once the decision process algorithm was elicited, it became clear that it had been over-engineered. (In reality, the stage identified would never be reached because other factors would have interfered long before, changing the emphasis and altering the decision process in such a way that an entirely different algorithm would be followed in practice). Although this indicated that effort may have been wasted, such occurrences were viewed as strengths and advantages of the approach adopted. During the development of the module on *commercial risk* (one of the major components of COMPASS), as a direct result of the primary expert having to resort to first principles in order to address over-engineering by other experts, the limits of the stability of the knowledge were identified, resulting in a far more robust structure than would otherwise have been possible.

The first area tackled was the *accounts*. There being a clear consensus on standard forms of the analysis to undertake, this proved to be the most straight-forward of all the areas addressed. Other modules followed with varying degrees of difficulty being experienced in the elicitation process—*viability, safety, commercial risk,* and *credentials.* Due to its emphasis on qualitative data—quality of management, manufacturing process, product, etc.—the greatest amount of work was on the *credentials* module.

The developers believed that the key to the success of the knowledge elicitation process was not so much the techniques used, rather the patience with which the whole process was conducted—the knowledge engineer's willingness to listen and the expert's willingness to keep working on it, frequently accepting that ground previously covered had to be revisited yet again.

Another key factor they identified that contributed towards the success of the elicitation process was their loyalty and trust in each other, combined with a deep sense of ownership of the project, particularly on those occasions when frustrations surfaced as it appeared that a major barrier had been encountered and that no progress was being made.

The final success factor was their adherence to a "keep-it-simple, keep-it-flexible" philosophy, Faced with a choice between a complex approach and a simple one, they always took the simple option, only retracing their steps and taking the complex path if it transpired that the simple approach was not feasible.

Thanks to the existence of these attitudinal factors, even the worst barriers were overcome and what had been foreseen at the outset as being a relatively simple system developed into a highly complex product.

3.3. Knowledge Articulation

The expert found that articulation of his expertise was very difficult:

Something like the lending process sounds simple, that is the belief. There are a number of processes involved in it *and* most of them follow some sort of logical pattern. So there is a vague *notion* that they are capable of *being* put into a rule-based structure. But, in real life the processes get muddled together and *you* do not actually work through things in that sort of sequence. Trying to describe the logic of your thought process is not very easy because you do not go about it that way.

Occasionally, others were brought in to fine-tune some of the knowledge. However, this was never particularly successful. Some were so enthusiastic that it became over-complicated. Others had no sense of ownership/loyalty to the project, which led to their dropping their input when something else came along. In contrast, much of the elicitation and development, especially in the early stages, was undertaken outside normal working hours at the expert's home or in his otherwise empty office.

One of the major contributors to the power of COMPASS was the expert's increasing awareness of his own expertise, and of the implications of this metacognition for the lending assessment process:

I keep wanting to do more things because I can now recognise how . . . [COMPASS] . . . can do more things. **Commercial risk** is a perfect example of something that, as a bank, we did not do very rigorously because we did not actually have any methodology for doing it. As the program has developed we have recognised that we actually have the processing capacity and the information requirement to enable us to do it properly, much more rigorously than we had ever thought of doing on a manual basis. There are quite a number of examples like that where the imagination is running far ahead of programming . . .

Another was the willingness of the knowledge engineer to question all assertions made by the expert and the willingness of the expert to accept he might be wrong. It ensured that nothing was incorporated within the knowledge base without first being examined and validated.

It is quite a threatening process, somebody coming along and demanding that you articulate expertise, because none of us are supremely confident in what we do. Life is about convincing yourself as well as others that you are actually competent. So the challenge of someone coming along and saying "so you really think that you are good at this—then articulate it" is difficult to respond to objectively. It is quite difficult for someone to challenge an "expert's" expertise in a way that minimises the sense of threat, makes you feel at ease, and allows you to work through it and, in fact, learn.

I remember being told that initially it would be a learning process, getting the knowledge out and into the system's structure; and I said "don't be ridiculous, I know what I am doing". But, in fact, that is the way it has turned out. It does improve the way you are doing your job. You do learn because it suddenly hits you that you have not been doing things properly. Bank lending is not a branch of knowledge that is defined, it is not taught in a systematic way. There is no right or wrong way of doing it. Within the banking industry it has always been regarded as a bit of an art—which, some would argue, has been a good excuse for people not actually determining what the rules are. And there is quite a lot of judgement involved in actually identifying and distinguishing those areas where you do need judgement from those where what you need is information and analysis and relevance.

The knowledge engineer's lack of knowledge of banking and loan assessment was viewed as having been a positive factor. His banking knowledge came from the elicitation process, which helped him to detect inconsistencies that another loan officer may have overlooked. There were disadvantages, but these were largely terminological—the "current ratio," for example, had to be explained at length.

3.4. Software Aspects

The identification of appropriate software was not a significant problem in the development of COMPASS. It was first developed in *C*, initially on a 286 DOS-based PC. In 1991, the system was rewritten for the *Windows* environment, programming modularization being adopted at that point, to ensure editing flexibility. By the time the working version was released for testing in 1992, the platform had moved again, this time to *OS/2*, bringing it into line with the *Bank of Scotland*'s IT development strategy. In Spring 1993, an object oriented approach was identified as appropriate for subsequent development and C^{++} was recognized as the appropriate vehicle. Work started on major enhancements and improvements to COMPASS towards the end of 1993. In 1994 COMPASS was recognized as a major IT platform for the Bank, incorporating data on customers and their environment with account information downloaded from the Bank's mainframe to a client–server architecture.

3.5. Training and Support of Users

Loan officers receive a minimal amount of familiarity training to ensure that they understand how to get into the system, access the appropriate screen, and enter information. This also includes training in understanding the output and in what they can do with it.

In addition, user groups meet monthly, in some cases fortnightly, talking about how they are coping with the system, and discussing their complaints and ideas. One of the results has been a large number of suggested changes to the system. This was expected. In fact, it was one of the reasons why loan officers were largely excluded from the development process: they are not only end users, they are experts in their own right and involving them in the development would have introduced all the problems of dealing with multiple experts (Turban & Tan, 1993), something that a conscious decision was taken to avoid from the start of the project.

3.6. User Resistance

Non-involvement of users in expert system development is liable to result in resistance and may lead to failure of the expert system (Moulin, Boulet, & Meyer, 1992). Yet, although use of COMPASS is mandatory for loan officers in branches where it has been installed, resistance has not been significant. Three factors may have contributed to this lack of resistance: the Chief Executive of the *Bank of Scotland* made it clear that use of COMPASS was Bank policy; users do have the option to make whatever decision they believe is appropriate, even if it disagrees with what COMPASS is recommending (though they would be required to justify their actions to Head Office); and the thorough testing in an operational environment that has eliminated any potential negative impact that might have arisen had there been any operational bugs in the system.

3.7. By-Product

In the course of the development of the COMPASS expert system, a shell interface was constructed which can be used to transport the COMPASS approach to other lending organizations. As a result, the COMPASS philosophy has the potential to enter the banking sector on a grand scale—within months of being installed in the branches of the *Bank of Scotland*, two major European banks and one American bank had expressed an interest in the product, with a view towards its potential development into a similar facility for their use.

3.8. Financial Costs and Benefits

Use of COMPASS has resulted in major improvements on bad and doubtful debts, increased efficiency in loan processing, less cost, improved loan structuring and pricing in relation to risk—all integral factors in contributing towards extensive financial benefit. It is anticipated that the cost savings generated by COMPASS over the coming years will provide the *Bank of Scotland* with a major edge over its competitors. (Goodall, 1994)

3.9. Non-Financial Benefits

COMPASS imposes control over the loan officers, yet it gives them greater freedom through increasing the level of loan facility they are permitted to grant without reference to Head Office. It also frees a significant amount of their time and it has already been found to be a very effective training device, loan officers having been seen to alter their thinking and general approach to lending as a result of using it.

It is not only the loan officers who have more time available as a result of using COMPASS, Head Office staff also have more time for other activities. In addition, the work Head Office now performs on individual applications is much more focused on the important issues.

Bank of Scotland customers have benefited from the significantly improved speed of response to requests for borrowing, which the Bank perceives as being likely to enhance its reputation and lead to increased business.

Changes in *Bank of Scotland* lending policy are now automatically incorporated immediately into all lending decisions. Related to that, the greatest benefit for the bank has been the consistency in decision making that has resulted from COMPASS providing decision support at all levels of the credit appraisal process.

4. COMPASS ARCHITECTURE

Typically, banks have spreadsheet models that perform data-mining-based what-if analysis. They extract data from accounts and construct ratios. Normally, at that point the loan officer will examine the ratios, decide whether they are "good" or "bad", and then decide what action to take. COMPASS takes the ratio results and refines them further. Using its encapsulated loan officer expertise, it applies the relevant knowledge from the end user (loan officer) in order to make recommendations concerning the lending proposal. The encapsulated expertise sits on top of the two traditional layers of information—the *Customer Information File* at the base level, which holds information on the customers and on existing agreements with the customers; and the *Accounts* level that deals with all the analysis and the modelling of the data (see Figure 1).

COMPASS is based on the premise that the main lending process takes place away from the financial data—that the traditional spreadsheet-modelling-based facility used in many banks is only a supporting factor in the overall lending decision process. Much of that process is based on other factors and it is these other

factors that have been incorporated into separate modules within COMPASS. Three key modules—*viability*, *safety*, and *credentials*—interact with an Accounts module within a two-dimensional control environment (module). Concurrently, customer-specific data (held in a *Customer Information File*) is filtered and assessed against environmental-specific data concerning the sector (industrial, geographical, market) in which the customer operates. (see Figure 2). At the end of each COMPASS consultation, a natural language report is produced containing recommendations to the bank loan officer on the customer's request for lending.

Under the traditional system, there is always a risk that the customer's enthusiasm for a proposal could interfere with the judgement of the loan officer. The *viability* module helps to maintain an unbiased view by guiding the loan officer through an assessment of the customer. It examines the potential for the customer to attain and support the projected activity—for example, whether the customer is likely to survive through the projected loan period. This assessment is underpinned by conventional ratio analysis undertaken upon the financial structure of the customer, its flexibility and strength, along with the quality and magnitude of its performance. However, COMPASS does so within the context of the *Bank of Scotland*'s knowledge of the sector (*sector environment*) in which the customer operates and of the Bank's attitude towards lending in that area, weighting values and outcomes accordingly.

One factor that the loan officer must attempt to address concerns minimizing the possibility that the Bank will fail to recoup its loan. One possibly confounding factor concerns the fact that, as with *viability*, there is a possibility of lending officer bias that could result in inappropriate security (*safety*) being attached to a

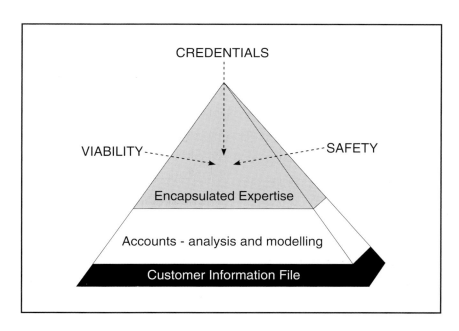

FIGURE 1. COMPASS.

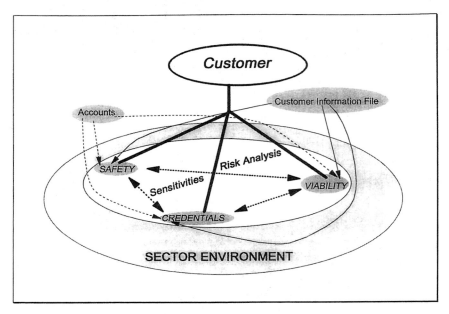

FIGURE 2. The COMPASS modules.

lending offer. COMPASS assesses the means by which the loan facility may be recouped (by, for example, evaluating the "true" worth of potentially secured assets) and determines the extent to which the lender can be "guaranteed" repayment no matter what occurs. As with *viability*, it does so through ratio analysis, but on the quality and magnitude of cash flow, the extent and quality of discounted assets and the extent of cover available. Again, this is done in the context of the Bank's lending sector knowledge: knowledge derived by creating a central knowledge base containing data and information on all the Bank's customers, including their management accounting data and projections. This knowledge base is updated daily.

The crucial variable, however, is the customer's *credentials*—how well is the customer known to the *Bank of Scotland*? A well-known and trusted customer may well be offered a loan facility even though either or both *viability* and *safety* are less than ideal. COMPASS guides the loan officer through an assessment of the customer's *credentials*, looking at the accounts information, management, manufacturing process, product, market, sales; and assists in arriving at an overall view of the three key variables so as to minimize the risk to the Bank; while, at the same time, ensuring that customers are not alienated by decisions taken that ignore their credibility.

For example, a customer that has a reputation for always meeting repayment schedules and for being careful in the manner in which funds are used may well be granted a loan facility even though *viability* is assessed as low and the level of security (*safety*) available is inadequate to cover the facility. By way of contrast, in a similar situation, but involving a new customer with no previous dealings with the *Bank of*

Scotland, the application would almost certainly be refused. This mimics the process previously undertaken by the loan officer, but COMPASS ensures that customer credibility is assessed objectively, consistently, and in line with Bank policy.

5. CONTROL ENVIRONMENT

COMPASS operates within a two-level control environment. "On-site" control is operated by the loan officer who, as the end-user, can perform sensitivity analysis on any of the data. For example, during the assessment of *safety*, the loan rate may be set to 5% instead of 4%. As the loan officer is likely to be the bank employee who usually deals with the company, the results of the sensitivity analysis can be assessed from that perspective. Consequently, through the consultation, the loan officer's own company-specific expertise is integrated with the generic loan officer expertise of COMPASS.

The second level of control is imposed by the Head Office of the Bank. They can change the same factors as the loan officer. However, they can also adjust the Bank's view of the sector (*sector environment*) in which the customer operates. This sector view acts as a back-cloth for the whole process. Changes to it can result in the loan officer's view of a customer altering dramatically from one day to the next, even though none of the customer-specific data has changed. As a result, the consultation process is dynamic, results altering daily according to changes in the sector environment.

Head Office control is also imposed through checking of the loan consultations. Each consultation is recorded and transmitted automatically to Head Office. Where the facility requested is below the loan officer's approval threshold, the loan officer may authorize the loan on the basis of the COMPASS consultation report. While Head Office may review such an application, they will not alter the loan officer's decision, provided it followed the advice contained in the report. (Loan officers may choose not to follow the COMPASS recommendations but, if so, they must justify their actions to Head Office.) Where the application exceeds the loan officer's approval threshold, or where the loan officer is unwilling to give the customer a firm response, the consultation report can be used to indicate to the customer what the likely outcome will be. Head Office will review the consultation and then inform the loan officer of the decision to make. This system mirrors the previous manual approach. However, COMPASS has led to the loan officers' authority thresholds being raised, enabling many more immediate decisions to be made. The time between the start of the consultation and the creation of the report is from 5 to 30 minutes, compared to over a week for the same process without COMPASS. The Head Office authorization process is also much faster; decisions, both by the loan officers and by Head Office, are much more consistent; and both the loan officers and the Head Office are now concentrating on the significant issues, rather than on every aspect of the application.

The main responsibility for the upkeep of the databases and the systems is at the account manager level, typically in the branches of the Bank. All new information (management accounts, for example) is entered onto disc at the branches and then uploaded nightly to the Bank's mainframe. It is then analysed, filtered, and distributed into the appropriate *customer information files* and sector knowledge bases. As a result, any new information on any customer becomes part of the sector environment for all other customers in the same sector within a few hours of the Bank receiving it. Similarly, information received from COMPASS consultations is filtered swiftly through to the relevant sector environments.

6. A COMPASS CONSULTATION

(See Figure 3). Upon receiving a loan application, the loan officer accesses COMPASS and enters the customer details. Information on the company structure, security, and existing borrowing is entered, along with account information down-loaded from the mainframe link. The audited, management, and projected accounts of the customer are also accessed. A seven-year span is maintained, three years historic, the current year, and a three-year projection. If the loan applicant is a new customer, COMPASS helps the loan officer to identify the customer's industrial sector from a choice of 17 primary sectors that subdivide into a total of 84 secondary sectors.

At this point, COMPASS accesses the appropriate sector knowledge base and takes the loan officer through the details of the proposal—what is known about the

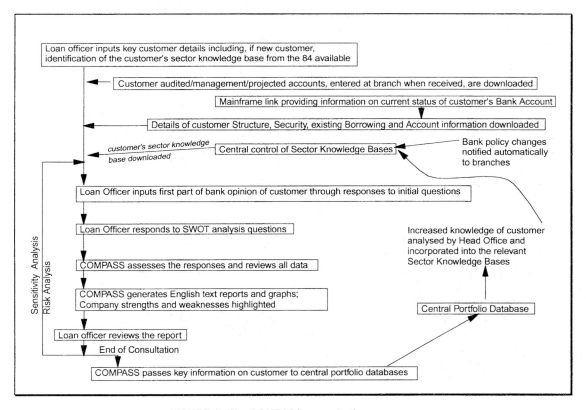

FIGURE 3. The COMPASS consultation process.

company, what the lending is for, and for how much, etc. These questions have a variable format ranging from simple "yes"/"no" responses (e.g., "has the board of directors changed in the last three months?") to five-point Likert scale responses.

It then administers a *Strengths*, *Weaknesses*, *Opportunities*, and *Threats* (SWOT) analysis comprizing a series of structured sector-specific questions that pass through the three key modules of *viability*, *safety*, and *credentials*. All these questions require responses on a five-point scale, running from one to five. There is also the option to give a "zero" response where the loan officer does not know the answer (see Figure 4). The SWOT analysis comprises a maximum of 70 questions, up to 14 on each of its five dimensions—Market, Sales, Management, Process, and Product. The questions and the number of them asked depend upon the customer's sector environment.

COMPASS takes the response to these questions and analyses them in order to assess the strength to place upon the loan officer's opinions, largely from the frequency of "zero" and "midpoint" responses. The weighting derived is then applied to the qualitative data and the resulting analysis is then combined with the quantitative data, all in the context of the customer's sector environment. Scale fluctuations between loan officers are being monitored (as part of the iterative

prototyping approach that has been maintained following the move from development to implementation) and, should any significant scale effect be identified, the heuristic will be amended accordingly.

Immediately upon completion of the interaction with the loan officer, COMPASS finishes its analysis, informs the loan officer of the strengths and weaknesses of the lending situation, and suggests the terms and conditions upon which lending ought to be granted, if at all. The advice incorporates the Bank's lending policy (in terms of pricing, conditions, etc). In addition, it indicates the areas that the loan officer should monitor, based on its knowledge of where the risks are coming from.

COMPASS does not tell the loan officer what to do. The output is designed to highlight strengths and weaknesses of a lending situation. If the situation were particularly strong, COMPASS would recommend lending. If it were very weak, it would recommend against lending. For the bulk of situations that are neither very strong nor very weak, it indicates where they are strong, and why, and where they are weak, and why. It highlights the risks, explains why they are risks and quantifies them, both in terms of the likelihood of occurrence and the movement required in order to eliminate them. This offers the possibility of an enhanced, more informative, more supportive service to customers. However, COMPASS has not been in use for a sufficiently long period to

Rating Form:	Strong 5; Weak 1; Unknown 0		
	Management		Page: 1
Strengths		**Weaknesses**	**Rating**
Strong Board (Collective Responsibility)		Autocratic	4
Wide Experience in Business/ Qualification in Main Functions		Narrow	3
Good Depth of Management		Key Management Difficult to Replace	2
Clear Strategic Goals		Undefined Corporate Strategy	3
Strongly Motivated to Perform		Rewards not Performance Related	4
Reliable and Comprehensive MIS		Poor Information System	0
OK	Cancel	Help	

FIGURE 4. Example of a completed management SWOT screen.

detect whether this has occurred.

The strength of COMPASS compared to more traditional approaches lies in its handling of these situations where, for example, there may be weak *viability* and weak *safety*, or weak *credentials* and strong *viability*, or some other unbalanced combination. It not only identifies weakness, but it knows the extent of the weakness i.e., the boundaries within which the risk exists. Under the more traditional approaches, while weaknesses were identified, there was no adequate way in which to test the limits of the risk. The loan officer had to make a judgement based on imprecise information. COMPASS clarifies the risk situation, making the judgement both easier and more likely to be appropriate.

The loan officer is then able to investigate the various risk aspects, using sensitivity analysis on the customer information data and sector data and, by revising the previous responses to any of the questions that had been presented by COMPASS, rerunning the *viability*, *safety*, and *credentials* modules. At any point, the loan officer may exit and request a report, seeing at a glance how the changes made have affected the conclusions drawn. Once the loan officer has completed the consultation, a final report can be generated based on the revised assumptions and responses[1]. As a result, while the final judgement is left with the loan officer (or, if the amounts involved are high, the Bank's Head Office), the decision taken is based on a consistently comprehensive methodology and approach that takes full account of the commercial risks involved.

7. CONCLUSIONS

COMPASS represents a new dimension in expert system-based decision support for bank loan appraisal. It has succeeded in capturing and modelling the inherent risk of bank lending and, as suggested by the opening quotation from Chorafas and Steinmann (1991), should give the *Bank of Scotland* a significant long-term edge over its competitors. Its strength lies in the combination of the encapsulation of the generic loan expertise of the *Bank of Scotland*'s senior lending officer; a sector-specific knowledge base comprising data and information from all the Bank's customers' management and projected accounts, as well as their financial accounts; and in the recognition that loan application assessment involves two categories of expertise—the generic expertise relevant to all applications (that is encapsulated in COMPASS) and the customer-specific knowledge of the loan officer who has previously dealt

with the applicant.

Analysis of the development process has revealed factors that contributed positively to the knowledge elicitation process—simplicity, flexibility, focus—and highlighted the importance and benefits of loyalty to the project and patience. All the factors recommended by Firlej and Hellens (1991) for successful knowledge engineering were applied throughout the project. The result is a highly successful operational expert system for a task that had previously proved impossible to encapsulate within an expert system. Clearly, COMPASS supports the hypothesis that the explanation for the present lack of lending risk assessment expert systems is due to knowledge engineering-related issues rather than to a lack of appropriate software.

There are many lessons to be learned from COMPASS, not just in banking, but across all domains where deeply buried expertise must be elicited if a truly useful expert system is to be developed. In a domain as risk aware as banking has now become, it can only be a precursor of a new generation of decision support, a new generation that may very well be built using the shell interface that was developed during the building of COMPASS. However, the greatest lesson learned is that knowledge engineering is a non-trivial and highly skilled task that, if accorded appropriate status, can make possible what has previously proved impossible.

REFERENCES

Bench-Capon, T., & Rada, R. (1991). Expert systems in the UK: From AI to KBS. *Expert Systems with Applications*, 3(4), 397–402.

Butera, G., Frascari, E., & Iacona, G. (1990). Parmenide: an expert system for assessing the credit of industrial clients. *International Journal of Expert Systems*, 3(1), 73–85.

Chorafas, D. N., & Steinmann, H. (1991). *Expert systems in banking*. Basingstoke: MacMillan.

Edwards, A., & Connell, N. A. D. (1989). *Expert systems in accounting*. Hemel Hempstead: Prentice Hall.

Feigenbaum, E., McCorduck, P., & Nii, H. P. (1988). *The rise of the expert company* (pp. 119–122). Basingstoke, UK: MacMillan.

Firlej, M., & Hellens, D. (1991). *Knowledge elicitation, a practical handbook*. Hemel Hempstead: Prentice Hall.

Friedman, R. (1989). Credit analysis automation. *United States Banker*, **98**(6), 58.

Gaines, B. R., & Shaw, M. L. G. (1980). New directions in the analysis and interactive elicitation of personal construct systems. *International Journal of Man–Machine Studies*, **13**, 81–116.

Goodall, A. (1994). Bank of Scotland's COMPASS. *AI Watch*, February, 1–3.

Harris, M. D. (1992). Natural language in banking. *Intelligent Systems in Accounting, Finance and Management*, **1**(1), 65–73.

Hartvigsen, G. (1990). KABAL: a knowledge-based system for financial analysis in banking. *Expert Systems for Information Management*, 3(3), 213–231.

Hartvigsen, G. (1992). Limitations of knowledge-based systems for financial analysis in banking. *Expert systems with applications*, **4**(1), 19–32.

Kelly, G. A. (1955). *The psychology of personal constructs*. New York: Norton.

Klein, M., & Methlie, L. (1990). *Expert systems: a decision support approach* (p. 481). Wokingham: Addison-Wesley.

Lecot, K. (1988). Using expert systems in banking: the case of fraud

---

[1]One of the anonymous reviewers raised the issue of how the incidence of iterations affects the probability evaluations embedded in the software—could the iterations themselves create a scenario affected by the very iteration process? This will be the subject of future research.

detection and prevention. *Expert Systems Review*, **1**(3), 17–20.

Moulin, B., Boulet, M. M., & Meyer, M. A. (1992). Toward user centred approaches for the design of knowledge-based systems. *Expert Systems for Information Management*, **5**(2), 95–123.

Shaw, M. L. G., & Gaines, B. R. (1983). A computer aid to knowledge engineering. In the *Proceedings of the British Computer Society Conference on Expert Systems*, Cambridge, UK. pp, 263–271.

The Economist (1993). Banking: new tricks to learn. *The Economist*, Number 7806, April 10th, Survey.

Turban, E. (1992). *Expert systems and applied artificial intelligence*. New York: MacMillan.

Turban, E., & Tan, M. (1993). Methods for knowledge acquisition from multiple experts: an assessment. *The International Journal of Applied Expert Systems*, **1**(3), 101–119.

3.6 The learning organisation

D. J. Skyrme and D. M. Amidon

The 'learning organisation' is one of those terms that has gained in acceptance over the last few years, especially in Europe. Our research found significant overlap and correlation between knowledge-based companies and the 'learning organisation'. Some interviewees saw one as part of the other (but a different one depending on where they were coming from!), some as related but different. Thus to Glaxo Wellcome and Anglian Water, their main initiative was a learning organisation initiative from which knowledge management has evolved as a key component. On the other hand, Monsanto and CIBC each had knowledge as a part of a balanced triumvirate of initiatives, while Skandia drive management through intellectual capital and see learning as a vital support. Whatever your perspective, though, our research found that applying the concepts and principles of the 'learning organisation' is an important ingredient of any 'rounded' knowledge management programme.

What is a learning organisation? There are almost as many definitions as there are of culture. Some of those that resonated with the views of our interviewees are the following:

> *The essence of organisational learning is the organisation's ability to use the amazing mental capacity of all its members to create the kind of processes that will improve its own learning capacity.*
> Nancy Dixon[15]

> *A Learning Company is an organisation that facilitates the learning of all its members and continually transforms itself.*
> Pedler, Burgoyne and Boydell[16]

> *Organisational learning occurs through shared insights, knowledge and mental models ... and builds on past knowledge and experience – that is, on memory.*
> Ray Stata[17]

> *Organisations where people continually expand their capacity to create the results they truly desire, where new and expansive patterns of thinking are nurtured, where collective aspiration is set free, and where people are continually learning to learn together.*
> Peter Senge[18]

> *A learning organisation is an organisation skilled at creating, acquiring and transferring knowledge, and at modifying its behaviour to reflect new knowledge and insights.*
> David Garvin[19]

One of the problems identified by several respondents is that the 'learning organisation' label has been misappropriated in several quarters. Often, it is identified with individual learning and even then applied to conventional training. Michael McMaster, a management consultant, says that use of the term implies that many organisations may be deemed by default to be 'not learning', which is patently not true. The issues, he says, are to improve the capacity to learn, and to apply the learning. The real challenge is to move these up from the individual to the organisation as a whole.

David Garvin, a professor at Harvard Business School, has suggested five building blocks of a learning organisation:

1 systematic problem solving;

2 experimentation with new approaches;

3 learning from own experience and past history;

4 learning from the experience and best practices of others (e.g. in benchmarking);

5 transferring knowledge quickly and efficiently.

He thus starts drawing a correlation with factors we have identified as key to knowledge management. In the methods to improve the learning experience and transfer of knowledge (Table 7.4) he gives several examples [...]

Table 7.4 Methods to improve organisational learning	
Aspect of learning	**Methods and tools**
Learning from experience	• Processes that force managers to review success and failure, e.g.
	• Boeing's lessons from developing the 727/747 and applying them to the 766.
	• Jamborees (events, exhibitions) where examples of best practice are displayed.
	• Post appraisal unit to review lessons of a completed project e.g. BP.
	• Lessons learned database.
Learn from others	• Benchmarking as a disciplined process.
	• Customer visits to see product in action.
	• Contextual enquiry (ethnography).
	• First delivery teams.
Tools for transferring knowledge	• Written reports.
	• Videos.
	• Presentations.
	• Site visits and tours.
	• Job rotation.
	• Education and training linked implementation.

Another group that has drawn the links between organisational learning and knowledge is Roth and colleagues at North Carolina.[20] They portray learning capabilities as complementing rapid acquisition and deployment of knowledge to create world-class operations (Figure 7.4).

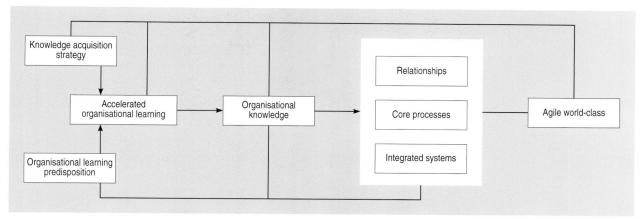

Figure 7.4   *Relationship of knowledge and organisational learning (Source: Roth)*

They argue that organisations need to understand how core knowledge drives their business – its philosophy, systems, approaches to problem solving and decision making – and how to develop the skills to acquire, organise, codify and deploy knowledge. They offer seven key principles:

1   A *learning philosophy* contributes to the development of knowledge around the organisation.

2   Improved *rates of learning* create more choices and opportunities; they need boundary spanning.

3   Adoption of '*stretch goals*'.

4   'Safe-failing', i.e. providing opportunities that encourage risk taking, but where damage from risk [is minimal] (see for example the use of simulation and games described above).

5   Systems for encouraging *knowledge and learning*.

6   Stimulating core *knowledge processes*.

7   Systems that *cross functional boundaries* e.g. teams and networks.

Fundamental to the new perspective is viewing products and processes in terms of their information, expertise and knowledge.

Another useful model is also provided by Nevis, DiBella and Gould, who likewise demonstrate the links between the learning organisation and knowledge, this time in a 'systems model' (Figure 7.5).

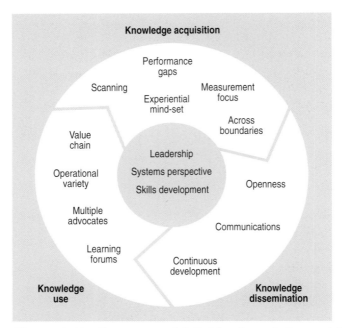

Figure 7.5 *Systems model linking knowledge and learning*
(Source: Adapted from: 'Understanding organisations as a learning system',
Nevis, DiBella and Gould, Sloan Management Review *(Winter 1993))*

Within the learning system, knowledge is processed through three stages. The diagram shows what 'facilitating factors' support the core knowledge processes of acquisition, dissemination and use. The specific 10 factors they listed fall neatly into the groups covered in this report and covered by architectural models and frameworks such as KMAT and EMSA […], thus:

- *Measurement* – performance gaps, measurement focus.

- *Processes* – scanning, operational variety.

- *Leadership* – involved leadership, multiple advocacy, continuous education, systems perspective.

- *Culture* – openness, experiential mind-set.

Throughout our research we found such perspectives being reinforced. Many of these factors have been discussed in previous chapters. Worthy of comment here are the two factors listed under process, which in our research were not as evident as perhaps they should be.

The first factor requiring more attention is sensing. The effective knowledge-based (and learning) organisation is one that senses and adapts to changes in its environment. The 'systems model' portrayed here emphasises the boundary with vital external knowledge, such as market and customer knowledge. This needs continuous sensing, and implies developing good market and competitor intelligence systems, as well as various interfaces with the external environment such as Steelcase's customer knowledge channel. Our sense is that many knowledge management programmes could benefit from a stronger orientation to developing these systematic sensing mechanisms.

The second factor is operational variety. The organisation that can respond better to change will need a greater diversity of responses. The explicit documentation of core business processes are often focused on the 'standard' process rather than the exceptions. This is where human knowledge and skill must supplement standard processes. A knowledge base should therefore capture this variety in its various 'cases'. We noted the example at CIGNA where additional knowledge and pointers to knowledge were encapsulated in the underwriter's workstation. The pitfall that knowledge managers should be wary of is that through the process of systematisation of knowledge, in the interests of efficiency and standardisation of formats, variety becomes diminished.

Five disciplines

It is appropriate here to review the role of Senge's five disciplines in knowledge management terms. As we have noted, Senge and colleagues' book *The Fifth Discipline Fieldbook* was heavily cited by our knowledge practitioners. Although the focus of this book is learning, explicit links are made to knowledge, for example:

'Learning in organisations means the continuous testing of experience, and the transformation of that experience into knowledge – accessible to the whole organisation, and relevant to its core purpose.'

The authors then pose these four questions:

1   Do you continually test your experiences?

2   Are you producing knowledge?

3   Is the knowledge shared?

4   Is the learning relevant?

In several places in the book knowledge is referred to as the 'capacity for effective action', in effect a collective capability developed through learning. But what of the five disciplines, where knowledge is rarely mentioned? Our views of how they relate to knowledge skills are shown in Table 7.5.

Table 7.5 Relationship of Senge's five disciplines to knowledge

Discipline	Contribution to knowledge management
Systems thinking – structures, relatedness, systemic (holistic perspectives); the specific methods of systems dynamics.	This discipline is about widening and deepening knowledge: 'seeking out interrelationships never discussed (or noticed) before'. Thus, systems dynamics helps people gain insights into what is often counter intuitive behaviour of a system (such as a supply chain). It's like Garvin's know-why knowledge.
Personal mastery – developing greater understanding of personal goals and today's reality, values and reality, interdependence with others.	This is self-knowledge. It is about making sense of your own position, by being more explicit. It is about articulating your knowledge in ways that are helpful to others.
Mental models – the models in your mind that shape actions and decisions. Two key tools are reflection and inquiry. Argyris's[21] 'ladder of inference' and action science are described, as is 'the left hand column'.[22] The most difficult discipline but the one with the greatest leverage, according to Senge.	Here the book makes an explicit link to knowledge. Mental models are 'the tacit knowledge in personal cognitive maps'. The 'left hand column' is 'what I'm thinking' (vs the right hand column: 'what is said'). The processes of enquiry and reflection aid the surfacing [of] tacit knowledge, making tacit knowledge explicit. This correlates with Nonaka and Takeuchi's 'knowledge spiral'.
Shared vision – This is the bringing together in shared processes of a collective vision – co-creating the future: 'bringing together multiple visions in an organic interdependent whole'. Dialogue is an important tool. The book described a shared vision as a tacit shared sense of purpose.	This is very much about knowledge building through knowledge sharing. It is moving personal knowledge into team knowledge and ultimately organisational knowledge. It requires a common language so that diverse perspectives can contribute to the overall whole and sense of purpose.
Team learning – Developing a collective understanding and capability, alignment so that the team acts as a whole. Unity since each member 'knows each other's hearts and minds'. Dialogue and skilful discussion are its two key methods.	This represents two aspects – the processes of tacit to explicit and vice versa, and the diffusion of individual knowledge to collective knowledge. It relates mostly to Nonaka's processes of socialisation, though to some extent externalisation.

There is thus significant correspondence between some of Senge's learning disciplines and those of knowledge processes described by Nonaka and Takeuchi.

We found organisations like Glaxo Wellcome and Monsanto applying many of Senge's techniques in the context of their learning organisation and knowledge programmes. Although our research shows growing awareness of the links between learning and knowledge, we suspect that most knowledge management programmes have yet to make these links explicit at the operational or technique level as implied by Table 7.5.

Lessons learned

An important explicit link between organisational learning and knowledge we encountered several times during our research was that of capturing 'lessons learned' knowledge. As shown in Figure 7.4, a key aspect is to accelerate organisational learning. It is essential to expedite the process whereby one part of the organisation, when it learns something of value, then makes this knowledge widely available.

We noted earlier that project assignments at several of the major management consultancies are not considered complete until participants have reflected on the key lessons and these have been elicited and added to their knowledge base. One difficulty reported frequently is how to get the stories and also how to portray them honestly. For example, Ernst & Young in describing Mobil's experience, tells of the difficulties of 'capturing the truth', since on the one hand they wanted to avoid 'bragging' and on the other 'there was an aversion to being associated with a "failure" of any kind'. In Mobil's case the lessons were developed in a shared workshop setting, that brought participants from several perspectives together.[23]

Garvin sets forth five conditions that should be present for organisations to learn from their past experience:[24]

1   Ensure that the learning is purposeful.

2   Set aside the time to conduct these activities.

3   Cultivate a culture that encourages self-assessment and critical thinking.

4   Create performance measurement and evaluation systems that recognise this and do not penalise employees for mistakes.

5   Build mechanisms to convert learning into policy and practice.

He outlines 'lessons learned' approaches that operate at several levels – individual, project team and organisation. They include the debriefing of skilled performers, post-project reviews and case studies. He cites the US Army Center for Lessons Learned as a good example of capturing and applying lessons learned at the organisational level.

Caselet – US Army

The 'lessons learned' approach

In the US Army no action or project is considered complete until it has been systematically reviewed. This 'learning after doing' philosophy started around 1985 and has now become established as an integral part of day to day activity in every unit. It is seen as part of a learning organisation system that equips the US Army for the constantly changing environment and battle scenarios of the

21st century. Known as AAR (After Action Review), its key features are:

- *Immediacy* – it starts as soon as possible after the activity; this may be at the end of the day in a battle situation.

- *All key people participate* – those in the front line as well as commanding officers.

- *It is done in a climate of openness* – full and frank discussion of experiences are encouraged (personal comments about individuals, while recorded in the experiences, do not go into an individual's personal record).

- *A set procedure is followed*, so that the process is easily remembered and reproducible.

- *It is recorded*, again in a predetermined format, so that lessons from different theatres of activity can be compared.

What happened, what was supposed to happen, what went wrong, how to reinforce success, and recommendations for fixing problems are all part of the review. Time is rigorously allocated as follows: 25 per cent for what happened; 25 per cent for why it happened and 50 per cent for what to do about it. This is deliberate, since the natural tendency is to jump straight into diagnosis and solutions without reviewing the past, which accounts for half the time in the AAR process.

References

15 *The Organizational Learning Cycle*, Nancy Dixon, McGraw-Hill (1994).

16 *The Learning Company: A Strategy for Sustainable Development*, Mike Pedler, John Burgoyne & Tom Boydell, McGraw-Hill (1991).

17 'Organizational Learning: The Key to Management Innovation', Ray Stata, *Sloan Management Review* (Spring 1989).

18 *The Fifth Discipline: The Art and Practice of the Learning Organisation*, Peter Senge, Doubleday (1990).

19 'Building a Learning Organisation', David Garvin, *Harvard Business Review*, pp.78–88 (July/August 1993).

20 'Knowledge Factory for Accelerated Learning Processes', Roth, Maruchest and Trimble, *Planning Review*, Vol. 22 No. 3 (May/June 1994).

21 *Overcoming Organizational Defenses*, Chris Argyris, Allyn and Bacon (1990).

22 *Theory in Practice*, Chris Argyris and Donald Schon, Jossey Bass (1974).

23 *Knowledge Transfer at Mobil: Using Success Stories for Organizational Learning*, Michael C. Beers, Ernst & Young Field Profile (May 1995).

24 'Learning from Experience', David A. Garvin, *Knowledge Management 96* Conference, Business Intelligence (December 1996).

Source: Amidon, D. M. and Skyrme, D. J. (1997) *Creating the Knowledge-Based Business*, London, Business Intelligence Ltd, Ch. 7, pp. 360–87

3.7 The new language lab – Parts 1 and 2

Johan Roos and Georg von Krogh

Part 1

In this and the following article Johan Roos and Georg von Krogh examine some of the recent thinking in management, in particular the application of epistemology.

The urgent need to understand 'knowledge-workers' and to create 'learning organizations' is an important preoccupation for the current generation of managers. But the challenge is daunting due to the lack of clear and useful frameworks for how knowledge is created by individuals – and within groups – engaged in business enterprises.

Epistemology is the field of science that deals with the creation of knowledge and we have found that it contains numerous insights for management that will accelerate the pace with which companies can develop and make use of knowledge. Three of the most powerful concepts within the domain of corporate epistemology are:

- *Self-reference*: the observation that each of us carries our own unique frame of references which is the source of both group creativity and group confusion. Because these frames are so individualized, you cannot 'force self-reference to happen through the exercise of authority; it must be voluntary.

- *Languaging*: the process through which we both create new meaning and share meaning and frames of reference in language.

- *Self-similarity*: when the same basic patterns of interaction re-occur at different scales within the company – individual, group, strategic business unit and so on. This is one of the key features of the most powerful knowledge-development processes and management systems.

What you see depends on who you are

Traditionally in companies, directions have been decided on and resources allocated very much as a parent gives guidance and boundaries to a child. A hierarchy of authority underpins this process.

The company chief executive gains the backing of investors based on his or her understanding of the commercial environment, the corporation develops a strategy based on this understanding and gets it accepted throughout the organization by virtue of its authority over the various businesses. In like manner, managers impose this strategy on their subordinates by virtue of their authority and so on down the hierarchical line.

Underpinning this process is the assumption that when exposed to a new experience, we all see it as the same thing. In the authority-based company, it really does not matter who gathers the data, does the analysis and/or draws the conclusions. The higher up one is in the hierarchy, the more information/knowledge one is supposed to have. So, with a higher position in the hierarchy came the privilege of strategic thinking.

Of course this does not reflect the needs of a business environment in which technology is creating new industries requiring radically new knowledge and skills. Nor does it reflect the strategic priorities of empowerment, organizational learning and foresight. Nor does it reflect that authority in companies no longer rests on a profound knowledge base that has been rigorously tested and validated throughout a long corporate career.

Self-referencing refers to the commonsense, everyday observation that each of us has a unique set of experiences that makes us see and react to things differently. What you see depends on who you are. Through this continuous self-reference we develop new knowledge that will always be unique to each one of us. In turn, our private knowledge makes us see new things others do not.

This is why it matters who did the industry analysis, who made the claim about emerging technology or who did the market segmentation.

Although the differences between people's views eventually converge and become trivial on routine matters, they are the essential building blocks for the creation of new knowledge. This is also why every company always develops an ever-changing knowledge base.

> [*Note by unit author*: as pointed out by one of the students who tested this unit, the key to this learning is the underlying assumptions that lead to the decisions taken, rather than the decisions themselves.]

While the exercise of command authority (where one individual tells another individual what to do) is sometimes necessary, excessive reliance on authority is an enormous barrier to the availability and creation of knowledge within a company. It prohibits individuals from successfully self-referencing.

Management also needs to understand norms, beliefs, values and world views of employees, groups, units and the whole company. All of those form the basis from which to see the future and to decide what new knowledge is legitimate and what is not.

This goes beyond alluding to vision/mission statements, job descriptions, organizational charts and other artefacts of the company. People participate in, and contribute their knowledge to, many organizations simultaneously, such as the company, the family and the basketball team. All of these experiences influence who they are and, therefore, what knowledge they develop and contribute to their companies.

Language as strategic resource

It is obvious that without language, knowledge could not flow from person to person within a company. It is equally obvious that if people speak different languages, then communication is stifled.

What is not always obvious is that due to self-referencing, people are constantly in the process of creating new language and new meanings, even if they share the same mother tongue. On the high value-added boundaries of knowledge creation, the ability to 'make' new language – and rapidly diffuse it through a company – is a strategic advantage.

The strategic significance of language is discussed in detail in [Part 2].

Making management simple so the business can be complex

Businesses are turning Frederick Taylor's rules of management upside down. Work groups are autonomous and decide for themselves how and when to fulfil orders; employees are multi-functional so that they can participate in different teams and work units.

This is a traditional manager's nightmare. Policies that are productive in one setting may be disruptive in another. In the extreme case, specific policies and action plans might need to be different for each individual worker. To the traditional manager, this looks like anarchy, like chaos.

The new-style manager looks for a hidden order behind the throes of knowledge creation. He or she takes a clue from the repeating patterns observed in nearly all things in nature. When patterns or processes re-occur at different levels within a system they are said to be 'self-similar'. The notion has been popularized by colorful pictures of geometric shapes – so-called 'fractals' – and by books on chaos theory, ironically enough.

But the good news for managers is that self-similarity seems to be nature's way of reducing one form of complexity while giving other forms of complexity – including knowledge – the means to flourish.

People, groups and companies have the capacity to self-reference and 'language' the way we have described. For example, if a company can simplify its management systems so that essentially the same process is used to make individual, team, business unit and corporate management decisions, then the artificial limits to the size or shape of that company might be eliminated, i.e., it can become as large or as small as it needs to be.

At the same time it increases the number of different markets in which a company might be able to operate effectively – all without increasing the complexity of managing the company.

This is precisely how a manufacturing and financial services company in the US has set out to improve its strategic management capability. It defines management responsibilities in terms of a small number of key functions: to develop new knowledge in the form of new options; to decide on which options are relevant; and to implement these options.

The model is designed to be replicated at any level in the organization. Middle managers use it in their daily activities as do foremen in the manufacturing plant.

Conclusion

In a knowledge-driven society where more and more employees are seen as knowledge workers, management is not what it used to be. In this section we have offered some 'food for thought' for a different managerial frame in the guise of three new concepts: languaging, self-reference and self-similarity.

These are old concepts; they have been part of human culture for tens of thousands of years. Still, they are taking on a new life as strategic tools in the hands of managers in the knowledge age.

The meaning of these concepts in management is not only about reassessing how we collectively and individually use language and stimulate self-reference but rethinking how we view power, trust and cooperation as well as how we develop foresight and set directions. On a more profound level, however, it requires us to rethink what is knowledge, how we view work and what it means to be employed.

One thing is certain: managers who have ability, guts and the humility constantly to reassess and challenge their management thinking and practice will be more valuable to their employers than those who do not.

Summary

Three of the most important concepts within the domain of corporate epistemology are 'self-referencing', 'languaging' and 'self-similarity'. Self-referencing refers to the everyday observation that each of us has a unique set of experiences which is the source of both group creativity and confusion. Differences between people's views are essential building blocks for the creation of new knowledge – excessive reliance on authority in a company is an enormous barrier to this process. Languaging is the process through which we create and share meaning and frames of reference. The ability to 'make' new language (and rapidly diffuse it through an organization) is a strategic advantage. When patterns of processes re-occur at different levels within a system they are said to be 'self-similar'. This seems to be nature's way of reducing one form of complexity while giving other forms of complexity (including knowledge) the opportunity to flourish. Artificial limits to a company's size can thereby be eliminated, the number of markets in which a company can operate effectively can be increased.

Part 2

The ability to create and diffuse language will be the key to the future of management.

Conversations are the backbone of business. Nothing gets done in a business without at least two people talking about it, and if they do not understand each other, things can go terribly wrong.

Every company has its own unique set of concepts and phrases – its own language – that cannot be easily translated or adopted by anyone else. Unless you are part of the conversations that made the language, and continually remake it, important meanings can be totally missed.

The success of a company in taking on a new product or market is directly related to its ability to create new language and rapidly diffuse it into operations. As Peter Drucker, management writer, has noted: 'Knowledge has become the key economic resource and the dominant, if not the only, source of comparative advantage'.

Since language is the currency of knowledge, it is the only means through which that advantage can be institutionalized and exploited.

Given the centrality of language to both the routine operation and the future success of business, it is ironic how few managers pay the slightest attention to it – or to the *conversations* that give rise to it. We have yet to see a strategic planning document with 'Manage the business conversations better' as a major bullet point, but the time has come to put it near the top of the list.

Strategic and operational conversations

There is a useful distinction to be made between the conversations that are primarily focused on executing existing routines within a business and those trying to create a space for something new to take shape.

The former covers issues that have been talked about previously. Perhaps these issues were new to everyone at some time in the past and once required more extensive conversation but not any longer.

The latter calls for people to move into new and unfamiliar territory, perhaps talking about things that have never been talked about before.

Operational conversations are about exploiting the knowledge gained in the past and present. Strategic conversations are about creating the knowledge – and the language to diffuse it – that will be necessary for a successful future.

[*Note by unit author*: conversations are the currency of knowledge within organisations. Tools exist to support various aspects of making sense of conversations and sharing them across an organisation.]

Managers instinctively seem to do a better job on the operational conversations than the strategic ones. Consider the following illustration: a general manager calls an afternoon meeting to discuss how to bring down the costs of maintenance on a production line. The discussion is lively and contentious but at the end a decision is hammered out and everyone leaves feeling like they accomplished something.

The following weekend the same group of managers gets together to talk about long-term strategy. The setting is a beautiful retreat center in the mountains; the company has spared no expense. There are long conversations about 'corporate culture', 'core competencies' and 'foresight' but the resulting statements feel fairly abstract and the managers' minds wander to a troubling employee or a contract that needs to be finalized. Most leave the meeting feeling that they wasted a lot of time and that nothing really will change.

This scene repeats itself with frustrating regularity. Managers who are proficient at talking about the day-to-day challenges in their businesses have trouble translating that success into their strategic conversations. 'Strategy sessions' end up focusing on day-to-day operational details or become over-structured, boring and political – a waste of time. The exceptions to this pattern are fondly remembered but remain exceptions.

In the days when a company's strategy took years to unfold and was tied to a fairly stable set of products, this limitation did not carry a great cost. Now they are under pressure to change directions in a matter of weeks or months. Like the obsolescence of computer equipment, a strategy has a very short shelf life. If managers are not proficient at talking about the future, their company will not have one.

One reason that managers have less success with strategic conversations is that they try to utilize the same rules and tools that they do in operational conversations. At first glance, one might think that the skills were transferable. A conversation is just a conversation, after all. Unfortunately, it does not work that way.

Managing strategic conversations

In most companies, operational and strategic conversations are two very different undertakings. Many common elements of operational conversations are in fact active barriers to successful strategic conversations. Managers need to abandon many of their well-worn habits and take a decidedly different course. This is not impossible but it takes discipline and attention to at least the following four basic rules:

Focus on building shared meaning, not on 'who's right'

In an operational conversation, a manager can request: 'Mary, make sure our new French client receives our standard marketing packet' without fear of being seriously misunderstood. This confidence is based on numerous conversations that have gone on before, both between the manager and Mary as well as a history of conversations among all the other workers before them.

Over time, the words and phrases develop widely shared meanings and a whole operational 'language' emerges that is as brief, clear and static as possible. There are clearly right and wrong interpretations of the language.

Newcomers are trained in the use and meaning of the language so that routines go smoothly. When people disagree, they strenuously advocate their own versions of 'the truth' to see whose version will prevail.

Strategic conversations have a decidedly different purpose. The future of the company does not yet exist; it must be created. The language surrounding the future of the company does not yet exist; it too must be created.

All of the conversations that will eventually give rise to operational routines have not yet taken place. There are no right or wrong answers yet. There is very little meaning that is shared. An executive may say: 'We must become a learning organization'. But everyone might understand the phrase in a different way.

If that fuzziness is allowed to persist, the routines that eventually result may not support each other and may even conflict. No one is right or wrong yet. Knowledge and perspectives must be shared before a powerful image of the future can be refined.

Strategic conversations must be a dialogue for understanding rather than advocacy for agreement. If an adversarial tone is allowed into strategic discussions then the creation of new knowledge and language will stop and the future shape of the company may turn out more like the present than it may need to be.

Leave authority at the door

Authority usually derives either from a manager's responsibility for a specific set of business operations (routines) or because an individual is known to possess a special knowledge to which others should defer. A general manager has the former, a technical expert has the latter, for example.

If a strategic conversation is sufficiently future-oriented, then it is impossible to know just what knowledge will be most important or what operational routines will result. Authority will be created 'along with' the future of the company, not beforehand. Managers who jump the gun and try to 'take control' will greatly limit what the future of the company might be. So while one's current organizational authority is relevant to operational conversations, it is meaningless to strategic ones.

As a result, as soon as authority is used in a discussion, it ceases to be a strategic conversation and becomes operational.

More extreme uses of power, such as threats and intimidation, are even less compatible with strategic conversations and may even be disruptive to operational discussions.

Keep strategy conversations exclusively for strategy

The incompatibility between authority and strategy makes it extremely difficult to mix strategic and operational conversations.

For example, the management team of a major newspaper once decided to set aside three hours for a strategy meeting. They met at 11 a.m. in the boardroom of the company, a very prestigious and beautiful room. At 11:10, everybody had arrived – well almost everybody. The editor-in-chief was still missing. The managing director of the newspaper suggested the meeting should start but the others indicated they would prefer to wait.

More small talk. Even more coffee. Everybody looked at their watches. At 11:20 the editor-in-chief arrived, red-eyed, furious and with puffs of cigar smoke following in his wake. He slammed the day's newspaper on the table and exclaimed: 'Have you seen this?!? Page two and five are completely missing. Our best stories have vanished. Our best advertisers have had their expensive advertisements erased. Who is responsible?' As might be guessed, there was no conversation about strategy that day. Attention shifted immediately to operational concerns. The next time a strategy meeting was called, people winced and came prepared to talk about operations. It does not take such a radical departure from the agenda to undercut strategic conversations. We have seen situations where an innocuous discussion about choosing a secretary, buying a new coffee machine or fixing a doorbell has had the same effect.

It is theoretically possible, of course, for an intensely knowledge-oriented company that is organized in a highly non-hierarchical manner to be able to blur the lines between strategic and operational conversations. But since most companies are still struggling with more rudimentary forms of decentralization, empowerment and shared decision-making, the exceptions to this rule are hardly worth noting.

Remove time pressure

Time is a scarce commodity in modern business and most managers typically seek a fast resolution to any discussion. Action is wanted, not words. If it were possible, some managers might prefer to eliminate conversation entirely, relying on the fewest possible words to communicate the desired results. Speed and efficiency are the watchwords of the operational environment and are in fact the goal of most operational conversations and language.

Strategy works to a different clock. Prematurely closing off strategic conversations only leads to poorer strategies and less successful operations. Ideally, strategic conversations have no 'beginning' or 'end'. The task of inventing the future of a company is on-going, and cannot be moulded to artificial deadlines. There is no simple rule to determine how much time is too much or too little.

The essential question, therefore, is how to use 'well' the time that is devoted to strategic conversations. The four rules above serve only as a starting point. Each company must invent its own best method of managing its strategic conversations.

The strategy of conversations

The development and diffusion of knowledge in a modern company are all about the development and diffusion of language. And the development and diffusion of language are all about the art of conversation. A word or phrase may embody a marvellous idea but it cannot really be called 'language' until it is successfully used in conversation with others.

The management of conversation needs to be a central concern of every manager who wishes to succeed in a knowledge-intensive age. The process through which we both create new meaning and share meaning and frames of reference in language is at the heart of knowledge development in organizations. It is a powerful concept within the domain of corporate epistemology. It is about the future of management.

Since the successful management of conversations still rests in the future for most companies, an interesting circularity arises: one of the first strategic conversations upon which a company must embark is how to engage in strategic conversations.

Without this knowledge and a language to diffuse it, there can be no progress. There is no logical way out of this loop, one must simply start talking about it – and talk about it as if the future depended on it. It does.

Summary

Language is the currency of knowledge and the time has come to put 'managing business conversations' near the top of the agenda. A distinction should be made between operating conversations (about exploiting knowledge gained in the past and present) and strategic conversations (creating new knowledge). Managers are instinctively better at the former. At a time when strategic shelf lives are getting shorter, though, not to address the latter will be costly. There are four basic rules. Focus on building 'shared meaning', not on who is right (strategic conversations should be a dialogue for understanding). Do not try to take control – current organizational authority is not relevant. Do not mix the two types of conversation. Remove time pressures and remember that strategy works to a different clock than operational discussions.

All this mostly rests in the future so there is an important circularity for companies. One of the first strategic conversations they will need to have is how to engage in strategic conversations.

Suggested further reading

Roos, J. and von Krogh, G. (1995) *Organizational Epistemology*, Macmillan.

Roos, J. and von Krogh, G. (1996) *Managing Knowledge: Perspectives on Cooperation and Competition*, Sage.

Source: *Financial Times Mastering Management* (1997) London, Financial Times/ Pitman Publishing, pp. 643–9.

Acknowledgements

Grateful acknowledgement is made to the following sources for permission to reproduce material in this book:

Reading 1.1: Extracts from *Accounting for Growth*, First Edition, by Terry Smith, published by Century Business. Used by permission of The Random House Group Limited; *Reading 1.2*: Extracts from *Accounting for Growth*, Second Edition, by Terry Smith, published by Century Business. Used by permission of The Random House Group Limited; *Reading 1.3*: Clarke, P. (2000) 'Shareholder value', *Accountancy Ireland*, Vol. 32, No. 5, October 2000, The Institute of Chartered Accountants in Ireland; *Reading 1.5*: Samuels, J. M., Wilkes, F. M. and Brayshaw, R. E. (1996) *Management of Company Finance*, Sixth Edition, Thomson Learning, International Thomson Publishing; *Reading 2.1*: Rutherford, B. (2000) 'When is a budget not a budget', *Accounting and Business*, 14 September 2000, Association of Chartered Certified Accountants; *Reading 2.2*: Kennedy, A. and Dugdale, D. (1999) 'Getting the most from budgeting', *Management Accounting*, February 1999, Vol. 77, No. 2. This article is reproduced with the kind permission of the Chartered Institute of Management Accountants; *Reading 2.3*: Reprinted by permission of *Harvard Business Review*. From 'Using the balanced scorecard as a strategic management system', by Robert S. Kaplan and David P. Norton, January–February 1996. Copyright © 1996 by Harvard Business School Publishing Corporation; *Reading 2.4*: Brabazon, T. and Brabazon, D. (2000) 'Benchmarking: does your performance measure up?', *Accountancy Ireland*, Vol. 32, No. 5, October 2000, The Institute of Chartered Accountants in Ireland; *Reading 2.5*: Dugdale, D. (1991) 'Is there a 'correct' method of investment appraisal?', *Management Accounting*, May 1991, This article is reproduced with the kind permission of the Chartered Institute of Management Accountants; *Reading 3.1*: Adapted from Lessem, R. (1987) *Intrapreneurship*, Gower Publishing Company Limited; *Reading 3.2*: Luthans, F. (1988) 'Successful versus effective real managers', *Academy of Management Executive*, Vol. II, No. 2, Academy of Management; *Reading 3.4*: Wilson, R. M. S. (1999) *Accounting for Marketing*, Thomson Learning, International Thomson Publishing; *Reading 3.5*: Sangster, A. (1995) 'The Bank of Scotland's COMPASS – The future of bank lending?', in *Expert Systems with Applications*, Vol. 9, No. 4, pp. 457–468, Pergamon Press. Copyright © 1995 Elsevier Science Ltd. Reprinted by permission of Elsevier Science Ltd.; *Reading 3.6*: 'The learning organisation'. Reproduced from *Creating the Knowledge-Based Business* by Debra M. Amidon and David J. Skyrme, © Business Intelligence, Third Floor, 22–24 Worple Road, Wimbledon, London, SW19 4DD, www.business-intelligence.co.uk; *Reading 3.7*: Roos, J. and von Krogh, G. (1997) *Financial Times Mastering Management*, Financial Times/Pitman Publishing. Reprinted by permission of Pearson Education Ltd.